# HOLISTIC HEALING

## GIFTED COMPASSIONATE THERAPY

*By Trauma Psychologist*

ERNIE L. VECCHIO

# Table of Contents

# Chapter One
# Introduction to Gifted Compassionate Therapy (GCT)

For more than three decades, I've observed people entering therapy burdened with invisible weights. They arrive armed with diagnoses—bipolar disorder, generalized anxiety, PTSD, depression—labels that attempt to encapsulate their pain but too often leave them feeling fragmented and misunderstood. When I ask someone—let's say Mary—what she considers her first diagnosis, she typically recites these labels one by one.

"Bipolar," she says. "Anxiety. PTSD."

I pause and gently prompt,

"What if your first diagnosis was simply Mary? Who is she? Where is she? Why is she?"

In this moment, her reaction is profound—her mouth drops open, and she replies, "My goodness. I've never thought of it that way before."

That moment is more than an insight; it is a recalibration. The weight of her labels begins to lift as Mary starts to see herself as more than a collection of diagnoses. For the first time in years, she reconnects with her identity, her humanity, and her innate capacity for healing. In that moment, she becomes energized, hopeful, and curious about the person beneath the surface of her struggles. This is the transformative spark that underpins Gifted Compassionate Therapy (GCT).

## A Paradigm Shift in Understanding the Human Condition

For too long, mental health treatment has centered on categorizing people—defining them by their symptoms rather than by their essence. Although diagnoses can serve as useful tools, they are often mistaken for the entirety of one's story. Research indicates that diagnostic labels frequently bring unintended consequences such as stigma, a reduction of identity, and the expectation of rejection (Hinshaw & Stier, 2008; Schulze, 2007). What if, instead of asking individuals to fit into predefined boxes, we invited them to reconnect with the truth of who and what they are?

In my experience, the most profound truths are often the simplest. For centuries, humanity believed the Earth was the center of the universe—a notion that shaped our understanding until the heliocentric model revealed a new truth: the Sun, not the Earth, is central. Today, we face a similar paradigm shift regarding our inner world. We have long oriented ourselves around the ego, treating it as the center of our being. Yet, the ego is no more the core of human experience than the Earth is the center of the solar system.

The true center is the heart.

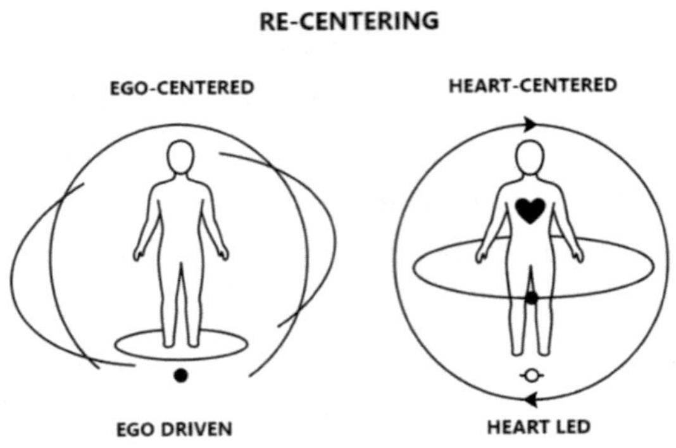


Gifted Compassionate Therapy is not about mere symptom management; it is about realignment. It recognizes that the human psyche is inherently self-corrective and can return to its natural state when distortions are removed (Vecchio, 2025). Just as the body instinctively heals, the psyche finds balance when the observer, spirit, ego, and heart function in harmony. This framework—outlined in *Holistic Healing: Gifted Compassionate Therapy*—challenges the prevailing symptom-focused care by offering an entirely new lens through which to view healing and growth. In Chapter Two, we will explore the philosophy of intentional evolution that underlies this self-corrective design.

Unlike many models, GCT does not elevate the ego to the status of ruler of human experience. Instead, it exposes the distortions created by ego solarism and invites individuals to re-center their consciousness around the heart. When people reconnect with their heart as their guiding compass, they move beyond ego distortions, reduce suffering, and reclaim their capacity for intentional evolution.

## An Invitation to Think Differently

This book is not a handbook for "fixing" brokenness, nor is it a reiteration of familiar therapeutic paradigms. It is an invitation to reconsider what it means to heal, grow, and thrive. Throughout these pages, you will encounter discussions that span from the intricacies of spiritual gravity to the emerging insights of neuroscience and the three-brain perspective. Each concept, from the observer to the heart, builds toward a comprehensive model of intentional evolution that you'll see developed in later chapters. I invite you to reflect on your own experiences as you read and consider: How might re-centering your internal compass transform your understanding of self?

## 1.1 Problem Statement

Modern psychotherapy often focuses on alleviating symptoms of human suffering but rarely addresses its root cause: ego solarism—a distortion in consciousness where the ego assumes the role of the human compass. Although designed as an adaptive mechanism, the ego frequently dominates perception, creating an artificial gravitational pull known as *spiritual gravity*. This distortion disconnects individuals from their inherent self-corrective design and obscures the heart's natural role as the center of human navigation. The result is pervasive emotional fragmentation, reactivity, and alienation from life as it was meant to be experienced (Vecchio, 2020, 2025).

To illustrate, consider how unresolved guilt, shame, and trauma magnify spiritual gravity. These unprocessed experiences trap individuals in cycles of reactivity, preventing them from engaging fully with the present moment. The ego, working through its four adaptive lenses—critic, bully, mediator, and counselor—assumes a dominant role in an effort to protect the self. Yet these same protective mechanisms distort perception, leaving individuals stuck in repetitive patterns of emotional pain. Over time, this disconnection intensifies, limiting access to both the observer—the neutral witness of experience—and the heart, which naturally guides clarity and alignment (Vecchio, 2020).

This disconnect mirrors a historic misconception: the belief in a geocentric universe, where the Earth was mistakenly considered the center of existence. Humanity's eventual acceptance of the heliocentric model, which positioned the Sun at the center, parallels the work of Gifted Compassionate Therapy. Moving forward, you will see how GCT seeks to re-center the heart as the guiding force of human consciousness, thereby restoring alignment and clarity within the psyche (Vecchio, 2025). Through the philosophy of intentional evolution, GCT posits that suffering is not merely a condition to be endured, but rather a catalyst for self-awareness, growth, and realignment.

On a societal level, spiritual gravity manifests in systems that reinforce fear, competition, and materialism. These ego-driven structures magnify disconnection and alienation globally. By addressing the underlying distortions in consciousness, GCT offers more than symptom relief—it provides a pathway to humane alignment, where both individuals and systems can thrive through reciprocity, compassion, and authenticity (Vecchio, 2020, 2025). In Chapters 4 and 5, we will introduce diagnostic tools and a practical framework to transform these challenges into opportunities for personal and collective evolution.

## 1.2 Purpose of Gifted Compassionate Therapy (GCT)

The purpose of Gifted Compassionate Therapy (GCT) is to restore individuals to their natural state of humane alignment, where the heart serves as the compass of human consciousness. Built on the philosophy of intentional evolution, GCT emphasizes the psyche's capacity to self-correct when freed from the distortions of spiritual gravity. By reconnecting individuals with their authentic selves, GCT reduces suffering, fosters emotional clarity, and facilitates intentional living (Vecchio, 2020, 2025).

The central aim of GCT is to guide individuals in exploring five existential questions that shape the human journey:

- **When am I?**
  This question prompts clients to examine whether their actions arise from *present reality* or are influenced by *reactive patterns from the past.* Recognizing the difference between immediate feelings and historical emotional overlays is key to breaking cycles of reactivity.

- **Where am I?**
  The heart, as the true compass, enables clients to locate emotional truth in the present moment without judgment. The practice of "looking with the heart" fosters self-awareness and strengthens connections to both internal and external realities .

- **Who am I?**
  While the ego is an adaptive tool for navigating external challenges, the heart reveals a deeper, authentic identity by aligning inner experiences with external reality. GCT invites individuals to embrace their true self, beyond egoic distortions.

- **What am I?**
  Before the ego takes shape, each person exists as a unified, intelligent, and observing consciousness. Reconnecting with this essence allows clients to access their natural expression and align with life's intended flow.

- **Why am I?**
  Human beings are here to live in reciprocal connection with life. Often, the ego, numbed by its wounds, acts as a parasitic consumer of experience. GCT helps realign the ego with the heart, thereby enabling authentic contribution and connection.

Through its diverse tools and interventions, GCT empowers clients to shift from ego-driven patterns to heart-centered alignment. It facilitates balance among the psyche's four components:

- **The Observer:** Offers clear, nonjudgmental insight.
- **The Spirit:** Drives growth and dynamic change.
- **The Ego:** Adapts to life's demands without overwhelming the system.
- **The Heart:** Guides with compassion and clarity.

By restoring this balance, GCT reduces suffering and fosters intentional evolution, enabling individuals to align with their purpose and thrive. As we move into later chapters, you'll see how these existential questions and the balance of internal components serve as a foundation for diagnostic and practical frameworks.

## Beyond Personal Transformation

GCT's impact extends beyond the individual. It challenges systems rooted in fear, materialism, and disconnection by inspiring collective transformation. Consider how, in education, GCT principles promote emotional intelligence over rigid performance metrics; or in healthcare, where a focus on heart-centered alignment encourages holistic, person-centered care. In governance, GCT advocates for policies grounded in equity and collaboration. By addressing egoic distortions on both personal and societal levels, GCT offers a roadmap for reconfiguring systems that have long sustained alienation and disconnection (Vecchio, 2020, 2025). This theme of collective evolution is revisited in Chapters 7 and 8, where real-life cases and systemic implications are explored.

## 1.3 Significance of Gifted Compassionate Therapy (GCT)

Gifted Compassionate Therapy represents a transformative approach to healing and growth by addressing the fundamental distortions in consciousness that perpetuate suffering. Unlike traditional psychotherapies that focus primarily on symptom alleviation, GCT shifts the focus toward realignment with the human psyche's natural design—where the heart acts as the compass, the ego is balanced, and suffering is reduced through intentional evolution. Its significance lies in its integration of ancient wisdom, modern psychology, and practical tools into a cohesive model that re-centers individuals in their true nature (Vecchio, 2020, 2025).

At its core, GCT posits that suffering stems from ego solarism and the artificial pull of spiritual gravity, which disconnects individuals from their self-corrective capacities. This disconnection leads to emotional fragmentation, reactivity, and alienation from life's intended flow. By re-centering the heart as the guiding force, GCT provides a pathway for accessing alignment through the interplay of the observer, spirit, ego, and heart. This holistic integration not only alleviates suffering but also fosters authentic self-awareness, emotional clarity, and meaningful action in daily life.

**Practical Relevance of GCT**

GCT stands out for its actionable tools. Clients learn to:

- Identify and diminish exaggerated ego states (e.g., the critic and bully).
- Reframe emotional experiences using the heart's lens to uncover present-moment truth.
- Break free from cyclical patterns by activating the observer's neutrality.

For instance, a client who experiences recurrent shame might apply GCT techniques to differentiate between ego distortions and the clarity offered by the heart. Shifting perception in this way allows the client to respond with compassion rather than reactivity, leading to meaningful transformation. In later chapters, we will delve into specific diagnostic tools and interventions that build on these foundational insights.

## 1.4 Mind-Body-Spirit: Outdated or Overly Simplistic

The traditional mind-body-spirit model has long served as a foundational framework for understanding human existence, emphasizing the interconnectedness of thoughts (mind), physical form (body), and deeper essence (spirit). While this approach has offered valuable insights, advances in neuroscience, psychophysiology, and trauma psychology reveal that this model is increasingly outdated and overly simplistic. Today, the emerging understanding of the three brains—the head brain, heart brain, and gut brain—offers a more nuanced and scientifically grounded perspective on human cognition, emotion, and well-being.

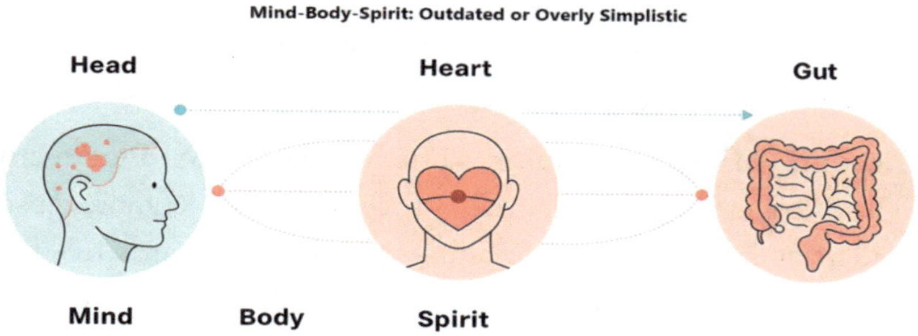


### The Heart Brain

Recent research underscores the concept of the heart as a "brain." Studies indicate that the heart contains approximately 40,000 neurons, enabling it to sense, feel, learn, and remember (McCraty et al., 2015). This complex neural network endows the heart with decision-making capabilities independent of the head brain. Dr. J. Andrew Armour first introduced the concept of the "heart brain" in 1991, describing the heart's intrinsic nervous system as a sophisticated network that shapes emotions and brain function (Armour, 1991). Organizations such as the HeartMath Institute have further explored how the heart brain contributes to emotional intelligence, coherence, and physiological balance (HeartMath Institute, n.d.).

### The Gut Brain

Similarly, the enteric nervous system, often referred to as the "second brain," contains approximately 100 million neurons—surpassing even the spinal cord. This system plays a critical role in digestion, mood regulation, and cognitive function (Furness, 2012). Dr. Michael Gershon's work in *The Second Brain* emphasizes the gut's semi-autonomous capacity to regulate not only gastrointestinal processes but also emotional states. The gut-brain axis has been implicated in mental health conditions such as anxiety and depression, highlighting the intricate connection between our digestive system and overall well-being (Porges, 2011).

**Beyond Mind-Body-Spirit: The Three-Brain Perspective**
This expanded model calls for a more comprehensive understanding of mental health—one that integrates the head brain, heart brain, and gut brain. In GCT, this three-brain perspective is essential because it aligns with the model's central tenet: re-centering the heart as the true compass of human consciousness. The heart brain not only validates the emotional wisdom central to GCT but also supports the notion of embodied cognition that we will explore further in subsequent chapters (Vecchio, 2020, 2025).

**Implications for Mental Health and Healing**
The three-brain perspective redefines our understanding in several keyways:

1. **The Mind (Head Brain):**
   Traditionally linked with logic, reasoning, and self-reflection, the head brain is now understood to operate as part of a broader network. Decision-making, emotional regulation, and intuition are distributed across the head, heart, and gut (McCraty et al., 2015; Gershon, 1998). For example, while the head brain processes analytical thought, the gut brain governs instinctive "gut feelings," and the heart brain influences empathy and emotional coherence.

2. **The Body as an Active Participant:**
   The three-brain perspective reframes the body as an active, intelligent system rather than a passive vessel. The enteric nervous system produces neurotransmitters that influence mood, while signals from the heart brain shape perception and overall emotional health (McCraty et al., 2015).

3. **The Spirit as Embodied and Integrated:**
   In traditional models, the spirit was often seen as abstract and separate. The three-brain perspective, however, reveals the spirit as an embodied presence (feeling, sensing, experiential self)—integrated within the heart and gut. Here, the gut brain represents intuitive knowing, and the heart brain symbolizes emotional depth and authenticity (Porges, 2011; Armour, 1991).

By embracing the three-brain perspective, Gifted Compassionate Therapy equips individuals with a more holistic understanding of their cognitive and emotional life. This approach provides the tools for trauma recovery, emotional regulation, and personal growth, thereby establishing this perspective as a cornerstone of holistic healing (Vecchio, 2020, 2025).

## 1.5 Navigating Resistance to the GCT Paradigm

As with any paradigm shift, therapists may encounter both internal resistance and external challenges when transitioning to the GCT approach. This resistance is not only natural but informative—often reflecting the same ego-centered patterns that GCT seeks to address.

**Common Forms of Resistance**

**Theoretical Resistance:** Many clinicians have invested years mastering traditional theoretical orientations and diagnostic frameworks. The shift from symptom-focused to heart-centered practice may initially feel like abandoning hard-earned expertise rather than expanding it.

**Practical Concerns:** Questions often arise about how GCT interfaces with insurance requirements, standardized treatment planning, and evidence-based practice mandates within institutional settings.

**Philosophical Doubts:** Some therapists may question whether concepts like "the heart as compass" are scientifically valid or whether they risk introducing spiritual concepts into secular therapeutic contexts.

**Personal Activation:** Perhaps most significantly, GCT invites therapists to examine their own ego patterns and heart disconnection—a process that can activate defensive responses and reluctance.

**Strategies for Navigating Resistance**

**Integration Rather Than Replacement:** Emphasize that GCT doesn't require abandoning existing therapeutic skills or knowledge. Rather, it provides an integrative framework that enhances traditional approaches by addressing their common limitation: over-reliance on ego-centered perspective.

Consider this dialogue with a CBT-trained therapist:

*Therapist:* "I've spent years perfecting cognitive restructuring techniques. It seems like GCT is asking me to set those aside."

*Response:* "GCT actually enhances cognitive work by adding the dimension of heart-centered awareness. Your expertise in helping clients identify cognitive distortions is valuable—GCT simply adds the question: 'What does your heart know about this situation that your mind might be missing?'"

**Empirical Anchoring:** Connect GCT concepts to established research in neuroscience, polyvagal theory, and psychophysiology. The three-brain model, for instance, is grounded in emerging research on neural networks in the heart and gut (McCraty et al., 2015; Mayer, 2016).

**Start Small:** Encourage therapists to experiment with simple GCT interventions alongside their established approaches. For example:

1. Add a brief observer activation exercise at the beginning of sessions
2. Experiment with heart-focused questions when clients seem stuck in analytical loops
3. Notice which egoic lens (critic, bully, mediator, counselor) appears most active in clients' narratives

**Self-Practice:** The most effective way to overcome resistance is through personal experience. Therapists who practice observer activation and heart-centered awareness in their own lives typically find that their skepticism diminishes as they experience the benefits firsthand.

### A Note on Insurance and Institutional Requirements

Many therapists express concern about how GCT fits within systems requiring diagnosis-driven treatment. In practice, GCT works effectively within these constraints by:

1. Acknowledging diagnostic criteria while reframing them as signals of misalignment rather than permanent conditions
2. Translating heart-centered interventions into recognizable treatment goals (e.g., "Develop emotional regulation through heart-focused awareness practice")
3. Documenting progress in terms that satisfy institutional requirements while maintaining GCT's holistic perspective

**Case Example: Therapist Transformation**

Dr. J, a clinical psychologist with 15 years of practice primarily using evidence-based protocols, initially approached GCT with skepticism. "I'm not comfortable introducing concepts that can't be measured," she explained. Her breakthrough came when working with a client who had made minimal progress despite years of cognitive interventions.

In supervision, she was encouraged to try a simple GCT approach: have the client place a hand on their heart while reflecting on their situation. The client's unexpected emotional release and subsequent insight prompted Dr. J to explore GCT more deeply. She discovered that integrating heart-centered awareness with her existing cognitive approaches created a synergistic effect, particularly for clients struggling with issues of meaning and purpose.

"I haven't abandoned my training," Dr. J reflected, "I've enhanced it by adding a dimension that was missing. Now when a client is caught in analytical loops, I have additional tools to help them access a different kind of wisdom."

## Reflective Prompt

As you begin your journey with GCT, notice your own resistance with the same compassionate observer awareness you'll cultivate in your clients. Each moment of reluctance offers an opportunity to distinguish between legitimate professional concerns and ego-driven defense mechanisms. Through this process, you'll not only become more effective in implementing GCT but will experience firsthand the transformative power of heart-centered awareness.

## Final Transitional Note

As you have seen in these introductory chapters, GCT offers a paradigm shift that addresses both personal suffering and broader societal disconnection. In the coming chapters, we will build upon these foundations. Chapter Two will delve into the philosophy of intentional evolution and the mechanisms of self-correction, while Chapter Three will expand on the foundational concepts—such as ego solarism, the alignment equation, and the five lenses of perception—providing the detailed framework on which GCT is built. Keep these core ideas in mind as you progress and consider how your own experiences might reflect the journey from ego-driven disconnection to heart-centered alignment.

# Chapter Two
## Philosophy of Intentional Evolution

At the heart of Gifted Compassionate Therapy (GCT) lies a profound philosophy: the human psyche is a self-correcting system, inherently designed to return to its natural state of balance and wholeness. This guiding framework—known as intentional evolution—reflects the innate intelligence of human consciousness, much like the body's remarkable ability to heal and adapt when provided the right conditions (Vecchio, 2020, 2025). In this chapter, we will explore in depth the foundations of intentional evolution and its role in facilitating the psyche's self-corrective processes. As you read, consider how these principles might inform your clinical work and contribute to both personal and societal transformation—a theme that will be developed further in later chapters.

*Transitional Note:*
Recall from Chapter One how we examined the distortions of spiritual gravity and ego solarism. Here, intentional evolution is presented as the counterforce that re-aligns the psyche, preparing the ground for the detailed clinical frameworks introduced in Chapter Three.

### The Core Philosophy of Self-Correction

Intentional evolution begins with a simple yet revolutionary insight: suffering is not a defect—it is a signal. Just as physical pain alerts the body to injury and the need for healing, emotional and psychological suffering indicates misalignment in the psyche. This perspective reframes suffering as valuable feedback rather than a condition to be eradicated (Vecchio, 2020).

Historically, the concept of self-healing is not new. Early physiologists such as Claude Bernard and Walter Cannon introduced the idea of homeostasis—the body's inherent drive to maintain stability despite external changes. In much the same way, the psyche is equipped with self-corrective mechanisms. Modern trauma research and neuroplasticity studies have reinforced this view, suggesting that the brain is continually rewiring itself in response to experience (van der Kolk, 2014). Intentional evolution builds on these ideas, asserting that when we create optimal internal conditions through awareness, compassion, and intentionality, the psyche naturally begins to realign and heal.

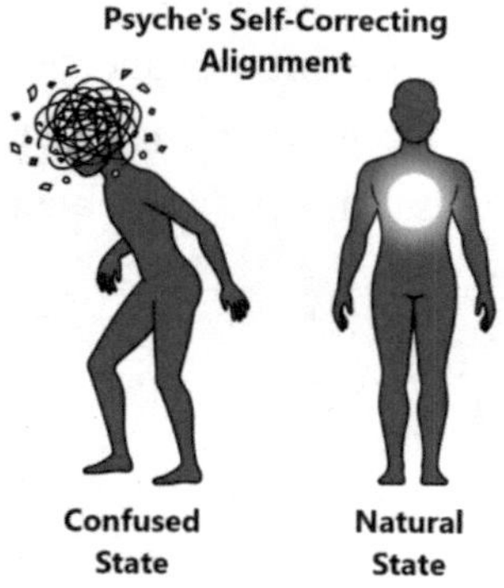


For example, consider a client experiencing chronic anxiety. Rather than simply prescribing medications to dull the symptoms, intentional evolution encourages viewing the anxiety as a "call to attention"—a signal that certain aspects of the self are misaligned. By exploring this signal, the client is guided to address the underlying wounds, leading not only to symptom relief but to profound personal growth.

**Summary:**
The core philosophy posits that, similar to the body's self-healing processes, the psyche is designed to restore balance when provided with the right conditions. Suffering is reinterpreted as feedback—an essential indicator that invites deeper self-exploration and growth.

**Reflective Prompt:**
Consider an instance in your practice where a client's emotional pain seemed overwhelming. How might you reframe that suffering as a signal for realignment rather than as an isolated pathology?

*Additional Historical Context:*
This shift from viewing suffering as purely negative to understanding it as a catalyst for growth also aligns with ancient wisdom traditions—from Buddhist notions of dukkha to indigenous teachings that see life's challenges as opportunities for spiritual maturation. By integrating both scientific and timeless insights, intentional evolution offers a robust, integrative framework for healing.

### The Mechanisms of Self-Correction

Gifted Compassionate Therapy identifies four key components that collaborate in the psyche's self-corrective process: the Observer, the Spirit, the Ego, and the Heart. Understanding these mechanisms in depth is crucial, as they form the foundation of the GCT model and recur throughout later chapters.

#### 1. The Observer

The Observer represents the neutral, higher consciousness within each individual. Functioning as a nonjudgmental witness, the Observer is akin to the mindfulness practice taught in many contemporary therapies. It allows clients to see their thoughts, feelings, and reactions from a distance, creating a space for clarity and reflection (Rogers, 1961). For instance, when a client is caught in a cycle of self-criticism, activating the Observer can help them recognize that the critical voice is not an absolute truth, but a distortion born of past trauma.

*Clinical Vignette:*
Consider Jane, who experiences intense self-criticism after making a minor mistake at work. By learning to engage her Observer, Jane begins to notice her automatic negative self-talk. Over time, she learns to step back from these thoughts, reducing the intensity of her self-judgment and opening a pathway to more balanced self-assessment.

## 2. The Spirit

The Spirit is the experiential core of our being—the raw, unfiltered sensor of life's experiences. It is the wellspring of creativity, passion, and vitality. However, when the Spirit is wounded—by rejection, fear, or shame—it can become entangled in past emotions and become *mean-spirited.* Healing the Spirit is therefore critical for restoring its positive, motivating force.

*Clinical Vignette:*
Tom, a client with a history of rejection, finds that his Spirit is often overwhelmed by feelings of abandonment. Through guided imagery and expressive arts therapy, Tom reconnects with the essence of his Spirit, transforming his raw emotional pain into a source of renewed creative energy and resilience.

## 3. The Ego

The Ego plays an adaptive role by helping us navigate the external world and form our identity. Yet, when the Ego becomes dominant—as seen in ego solarism—it distorts perception and fosters reactive patterns. For example, the Ego might magnify self-criticism or defensive behaviors, ultimately trapping the individual in cycles of internal conflict. GCT's approach is to recalibrate the Ego so that it functions as a supportive ally rather than a controlling force.

*Clinical Vignette:*
Sarah struggles with an overactive Ego that constantly compares her to others, leading to persistent feelings of inadequacy. Through cognitive reframing and mindfulness exercises, she learns to moderate her Ego's reactivity. As she reconnects with her Heart, Sarah discovers that her Ego can support her journey rather than undermine it.

**4. The Heart**

The Heart is the compass of human consciousness. It integrates emotional, cognitive, and intuitive insights, guiding us toward authenticity and balance. Re-centering on the Heart is essential for counteracting spiritual gravity—the false pull exerted by an overactive Ego. When the Heart is aligned, it provides the clarity and ethical guidance needed for true healing (Vecchio, 2025).

*Clinical Vignette:*
Michael, feeling lost after a career setback, finds that his decision-making is clouded by fear and self-doubt. In therapy, he is encouraged to "listen to his Heart"—to reconnect with his inner sense of purpose and integrity. Gradually, Michael experiences a renewed clarity that transforms his approach to both personal and professional challenges.

**Summary:**
The self-corrective mechanisms of the psyche depend on the harmonious interplay of the Observer, Spirit, Ego, and Heart. Each plays a unique role: the Observer creates reflective space; the Spirit fuels growth; the Ego, when balanced, helps navigate challenges; and the Heart offers the true compass for alignment.

**Reflective Prompt:**
How can you incorporate practices that help clients strengthen each of these components? Consider a simple mindfulness exercise to activate the Observer, or guided self-reflection to soothe the Spirit.

*Additional Elaboration:*
Therapeutic techniques such as mindfulness meditation, expressive art therapy, and cognitive reframing are all practical methods to enhance these self-corrective mechanisms. By understanding and nurturing these elements, clients can gradually transform suffering into an opportunity for growth and healing.

## Alignment as a Natural State

Alignment is not a state that must be forced—it is the natural condition of the psyche when the Observer, Spirit, Ego, and Heart operate in harmonious balance. This state is characterized by clarity, emotional regulation, and purposeful action. In contrast, an unnatural state—marked by an overactive, dominant Ego—results in fragmentation, reactivity, and disconnection from one's true self.

Intentional evolution posits that the Heart, not the Ego, should serve as the guiding compass of human consciousness. When distortions are removed, the natural state of alignment emerges. This balanced condition empowers individuals to process emotions effectively, make decisions in line with their values, and engage with life fully (Vecchio, 2020, 2025).

**Alignment Equations:**

- **Natural State:**
  $E + Hc = \downarrow S$
  (Nominal Ego + Heart as Compass = Decreased Suffering)
- **Unnatural State: (Egosolarism -weight where there is none = Spiritual Gravity)**
  $E^2 - Hc = \uparrow S$
  (Exaggerated Ego - Heart as Compass = Increased Suffering)

These equations encapsulate the impact of internal balance versus imbalance. When the Ego is regulated and the Heart leads, suffering decreases; conversely, when the Ego dominates, suffering is amplified.

**Expanded Discussion:**
The notion of alignment extends into every facet of life—from decision-making and interpersonal relationships to overall mental health. When clients operate from an aligned state, they are not merely symptom-free; they experience a renewed sense of purpose and authenticity. This transformation is what GCT ultimately seeks to cultivate.

**Summary:**
Alignment represents the innate, balanced state of the psyche. GCT's task is to reveal and support this state by harmonizing the interplay between the Observer, Spirit, Ego, and Heart.

**Reflective Prompt:**
Reflect on a moment when you experienced inner alignment. How did this state influence your decision-making and emotional

well-being? How might these insights inform your therapeutic practice?

**Transforming Suffering: Matter of the Heart**

A critical component of intentional evolution is the understanding that suffering, when processed intentionally, can serve as a catalyst for profound transformation. Gifted Compassionate Therapy posits that every experience of suffering contributes to "matter of the heart"—a reservoir of emotional and psychological material that, when engaged with, yields two vital byproducts: salt and oil.

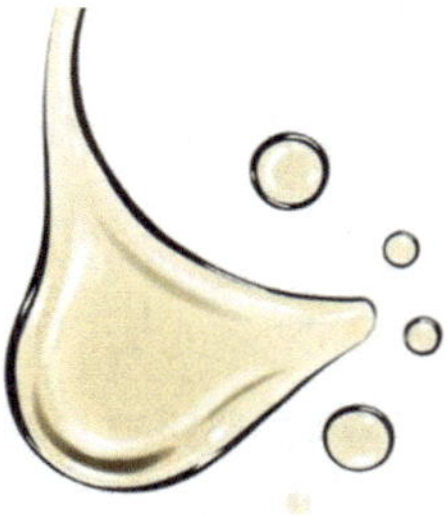

**Salt as Wisdom**

Salt is formed under immense pressure and serves as a preservative, capturing essential elements over time. In the context of the psyche, salt represents the wisdom distilled from suffering. It encapsulates the lessons learned through hardship and preserves them as insights that guide future growth (Vecchio, 2025). Consider how, over years, a person who has experienced significant loss might develop a deep capacity for empathy and understanding—this is the salt of life, the crystallized essence of hard-won wisdom.

**Oil as Healing Essence**

Oil functions as a lubricant that reduces friction. Metaphorically, oil symbolizes the healing energy that softens the tension between the Ego and the Spirit. When suffering is approached with humility and self-compassion, it produces this "lubricant" that enables smoother integration and transformation. Just as synovial fluid protects and eases movement in our joints, oil eases the internal tension, facilitating the transition from resistance to alignment.

**Clinical Applications: Salt and Oil in Therapeutic Dialogue**

These metaphors of salt and oil provide therapists with powerful language to help clients reframe their suffering and access their inner resources. The following clinical examples demonstrate how these concepts can be incorporated into therapeutic exchanges.

**Example 1: Transforming Long-term Grief into Wisdom**

**Context:** James, a 42-year-old teacher, entered therapy struggling with unresolved grief five years after losing his wife to cancer. His initial presentation included social withdrawal, emotional numbness, and a sense that his suffering had no purpose.

**Therapist:** "You've carried this grief for five years now, and it feels like it hasn't changed or served any purpose."

**Client:** "It just sits there. Heavy. Useless. It doesn't get better."

**Therapist:** "I'm wondering if we might look at your grief differently. In ancient times, salt was incredibly valuable—it preserved what was essential and gave flavor to life. It was formed through intense pressure, much like what you've experienced."

**Client:** "But how does my pain preserve anything? It just hurts."

**Therapist:** "That's a fair question. What I notice is how your experience has given you a depth I rarely see in others. Last week, you mentioned how you responded to your student who lost his grandfather—you knew exactly what to say and what not to say."

**Client:** *(reflective)* "I did know. I remember thinking no one could have told me those things if they hadn't been through it themselves."

**Therapist:** "That's the salt—the wisdom distilled from your suffering. It's preserved something essential about human connection that you now carry for others. It doesn't make the loss 'worth it,' but it means the suffering has transformed into something with value."

**Client:** "I never thought about it that way. There is a kind of knowing that came from this..."

**Therapist:** "Over the coming weeks, I'd like us to notice other ways this 'salt' appears in your life—how your experience has given you wisdom that now serves both you and others."

In subsequent sessions, James began identifying specific insights his grief had taught him—about resilience, about being present with others in pain, about appreciating moments of joy when they appeared. The metaphor helped him reconceptualize his suffering not as meaningless pain but as a difficult process that had yielded valuable wisdom.

**Example 2: Finding Self-Compassion After Divorce**

**Context:** Elena, a 38-year-old executive, sought therapy after a painful divorce. She was highly critical of herself for "failing" at marriage and displayed rigid perfectionism in her attempts to rebuild her life. Her internal friction was evident in persistent tension headaches and insomnia.

**Therapist:** "You've been working so hard to move forward, yet there's this constant friction between where you are and where you think you 'should' be."

**Client:** "I just can't accept that I'm still struggling with this. It's been over a year."

**Therapist:** "I'm wondering if something important might be missing in your approach. When mechanical parts rub against each other with no lubrication, they create heat, wear down, and eventually break. What's missing is oil."

**Client:** "What do you mean?"

**Therapist:** "Oil is what allows movement without damage. In our inner lives, that oil is self-compassion—the ability to acknowledge our pain without judgment. I notice that when you talk about your divorce, there's very little oil present. There's understanding for your ex-husband's limitations, even for your friends who've drifted away, but very little gentleness toward yourself."

**Client:** *(tearing up)* "I don't know how to be gentle with myself about this. It feels like letting myself off the hook."

**Therapist:** "Actually, oil doesn't remove accountability—it simply allows movement without destruction. Could we experiment with adding just a drop of this oil to your thoughts about the divorce?"

**Client:** "I can try. What would that look like?"

**Therapist:** "Perhaps something like: 'This divorce has been incredibly painful, and I'm doing the best I can to heal from it.'"

**Client:** *(repeats phrase, voice softening)* "That actually feels... different. Less tight."

**Therapist:** "That's the oil beginning to work. Notice how it doesn't change the facts of your situation, but it changes how you move through them. Your shoulders just dropped an inch."

**Client:** "I just felt something release in my chest."

**Therapist:** "That's what oil does—it reduces friction. As we continue our work together, we'll keep noticing where you need this kind of self-compassion to help you move through difficult emotions without tearing yourself apart."

Over time, Elena developed a practice of intentionally "applying oil" when she noticed self-criticism arising. She would place a hand on her heart and offer herself the same compassion she would offer a friend. This practice gradually reduced her insomnia and tension headaches, as the internal conflict between her critic and her authentic self began to ease.

**Example 3: Processing Childhood Neglect in Real Time**

**Context:** Michael, a 34-year-old artist, was processing childhood emotional neglect that had left him feeling chronically empty and disconnected. During one particularly emotional session, he accessed deep sadness about moments when his emotional needs were dismissed.

**Therapist:** *(noticing client's emotional breakthrough)* "Stay with this feeling if you can, Michael. There's something important happening right now."

**Client:** *(tearful)* "It hurts so much to feel how alone I was. But something's different... it's like I can feel the pain but also watch it at the same time."

**Therapist:** "That's your observer activated. As you stay with this experience, I'm wondering if you can notice what's happening in your body."

**Client:** "My chest feels open, raw... but also warmer somehow."

**Therapist:** "You're experiencing both aspects of transformation in this moment. The salt is forming—the wisdom and insight that comes from fully acknowledging what happened to you. And simultaneously, there's oil being produced—the compassion arising as you witness your younger self with new awareness."

**Client:** "It's strange. I've avoided this feeling for so long, but now that I'm in it, there's something almost... sacred about it."

**Therapist:** "That sacred quality is what happens when suffering is fully witnessed. The pain doesn't disappear, but it transforms. The salt preserves the truth of your experience, while the oil allows you to hold it without being torn apart by it."

**Client:** "I feel more... real... than I have in years."

**Therapist:** "This is the alchemy of intentional evolution—the transformation of raw suffering into wisdom and healing. Let's continue to notice what emerges as we hold this space together."

In this real-time example, the metaphors of salt and oil helped Michael conceptualize what was happening as he processed long-avoided emotions. Rather than being overwhelmed by pain, he could recognize the dual aspects of his experience—the crystallization of insight and the emergence of self-compassion. This framework allowed him to stay present with difficult emotions long enough for transformation to occur.

---

These clinical examples demonstrate how the metaphors of salt and oil can be woven into therapeutic dialogue to help clients reframe their suffering. By offering these concrete images, therapists provide clients with a language for understanding their experiences and a framework for transforming pain into resources for growth. The metaphors work not just as intellectual concepts but as experiential guides that help clients recognize and participate in their own healing process.

The power of these metaphors lies in their ability to shift clients from passive victims of suffering to active participants in transformation. Salt honors the hard-won wisdom that emerges from life's challenges, while oil acknowledges the healing power of self-compassion. Together, they offer a balanced approach that neither dismisses pain nor remains trapped within it.

**Extended Analogy:**
Imagine a vast salt mine where, over centuries, pressure transforms raw rock into valuable crystals. Similarly, our life experiences—when engaged with consciously—transform raw pain into wisdom. Likewise, think of oil extracted from ancient reserves that not only fuels engines but also lubricates them for efficient performance. In our inner world, oil represents that dynamic energy which allows us to move beyond the confines of an overactive Ego.

**Summary:**
The metaphors of salt and oil demonstrate that suffering, when transformed through intentional engagement, becomes a resource. Salt embodies the wisdom garnered from life's challenges, while oil symbolizes the healing essence that facilitates smooth internal realignment.

**Reflective Prompt:**
Consider a challenging experience from your own life or clinical work. What "salt" (wisdom) might be drawn from that experience? How could you help clients identify and harness the "oil" (healing energy) embedded within their pain?

*Additional Reflection:*
This transformative process is not about glorifying suffering but

about recognizing its potential. By reconfiguring the way we relate to pain, we open up new pathways for growth that are both personal and universal. In doing so, we honor the full spectrum of human experience.

## Practical Application in Therapy

The theoretical principles of intentional evolution gain their fullest meaning when applied in clinical settings. GCT translates these abstract ideas into concrete interventions that help clients tap into their self-corrective capacities.

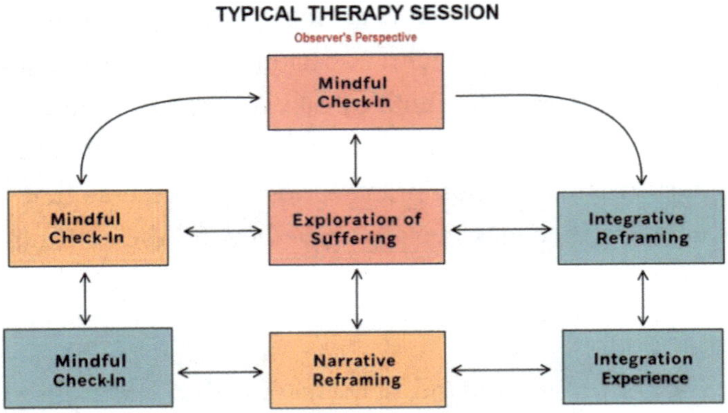


## Detailed Session Outline

Imagine a typical therapy session structured around these principles:

1. **Introduction and Mindful Check-In:**
   Begin with a brief mindfulness exercise designed to activate the Observer. This might involve guided breathing or a short meditation to bring clients into the present moment.

2. **Exploration of Suffering:**
   Invite the client to describe a recent challenging experience. Encourage them to articulate not only the pain but also the underlying emotions and thoughts—thereby identifying the "matter of the heart."

3. **Reflection and Narrative Reframing:**
   Guide the client in a narrative exercise where they reframe the experience. Ask questions such as, "What have you learned from this experience?" or "How might this pain be transformed into wisdom (salt)?" Encourage them to consider how self-compassion can act as oil, easing the transition from pain to growth.

4. **Integration and Action:**
   Conclude with a plan for integrating these insights into daily life. This may include setting small, actionable goals that align with the Heart's guidance. For example, if a client recognizes that fear is holding them back, they might set an intention to approach a feared situation gradually, using self-compassion as a support.

**Group and Community Applications**

Beyond individual sessions, these principles can be applied in group therapy or community workshops. For example, a workshop on "Transforming Suffering into Growth" could incorporate guided journaling, group discussion, and interactive exercises that help participants collectively explore the salt and oil metaphors.

**Summary:**
GCT transforms theory into practice by offering structured interventions that help clients reflect on their experiences, extract wisdom, and apply healing strategies. Whether in one-on-one

sessions or group settings, these practical applications are designed to unlock the self-corrective power of the psyche.

**Reflective Prompt:**
How can you integrate these session components into your current practice? Consider designing a pilot workshop that uses these techniques to help clients process and transform their suffering.

### Integration and Synthesis

To bring together the diverse elements of intentional evolution, this section synthesizes the core philosophy, mechanisms of self-correction, the transformative metaphors of salt and oil, and the practical applications into a unified framework.

Intentional evolution teaches us that suffering is not an end but a signal—a call for the psyche to self-correct. When the Observer, Spirit, Ego, and Heart are in balance, the natural state of alignment emerges, characterized by clarity, resilience, and purposeful action. This state is the goal of GCT, a state that is accessible through thoughtful reflection, deliberate practice, and compassionate intervention.

As you integrate these concepts into your work, reflect on how each element interacts:

- How does the Observer facilitate awareness?
- In what ways can the Spirit's raw energy be transformed when properly nurtured?
- How can the Ego be recalibrated to support, rather than obstruct, growth?

- And finally, how does the Heart serve as the unwavering guide toward alignment?

**Future Directions and Clinical Implications:**
Looking ahead, further research on neuroplasticity, heart coherence, and trauma-informed care will continue to enrich and validate these concepts. The framework of intentional evolution not only offers immediate clinical utility but also sets the stage for evolving therapeutic practices that honor the full complexity of human experience.

**Reflective Prompt:**
In what ways do these integrated concepts challenge or affirm your current therapeutic approach? How might you adapt your practice to incorporate the idea that every moment of suffering carries the seed of growth?

**Conclusion and Transitional Note**

The philosophy of intentional evolution reframes suffering as constructive feedback and affirms that the human psyche is designed to self-correct. Through an in-depth exploration of the core philosophy, mechanisms of self-correction, and the transformative metaphors of salt and oil, Gifted Compassionate Therapy provides a comprehensive roadmap for healing and growth. This chapter has laid the theoretical foundation upon which GCT is built, demonstrating that alignment is not an external achievement but an inherent state waiting to be revealed.

In Chapter Three. There, you will encounter a detailed clinical framework—including discussions of ego solarism, the alignment equation, and the five lenses of perception—that builds on these ideas to offer integrative, actionable tools for realigning the psyche.

# Chapter Three
# Egosolarism to Heart-Centered Healing

### The Algorithm of Intentional Evolution

In our journey toward holistic healing, one of the most transformative shifts is the recognition that the human psyche is not a static repository of fixed identities but a dynamic, self-correcting system. For too long, the prevailing model of mental health has centered on the ego—a necessary adaptive function that, over time, has mistaken itself for the nucleus of human existence. This phenomenon, which I call "ego-solarism," reflects a state in which an exaggerated, unchecked ego amplifies suffering by distorting perception and misinterpreting experience. Yet within Gifted Compassionate Therapy (GCT) lies a revolutionary alternative: a recalibration that places the heart at the center of our being. This chapter presents an integrative model—a healing algorithm that embodies the principle of intentional evolution, guiding us from an ego-dominated state toward a balanced, heart-centered existence.

At its core, this model can be succinctly expressed through a simple equation: when the ego operates in isolation and exaggerates its influence, suffering increases; mathematically, this can be described as $E^2 - Hc = \uparrow S$, where E represents the ego, Hc the heart as a compass, and S the resulting suffering. Conversely, when the ego is moderated and aligned with the heart, the equation becomes $E' + Hc = \downarrow S$, indicating that suffering diminishes when our inner compass—our heart—guides our actions. This algorithm is not just a mathematical abstraction; it is a practical roadmap for realigning the psyche, one that underscores the self-corrective nature of human consciousness.

**A recalibration that places the heart at the center of our being...**

From the earliest moments of life, the human body is designed to seek homeostasis. It adjusts, adapts, and heals, striving to maintain balance despite external challenges. The psyche, too, is endowed with this inherent drive for equilibrium. Yet, over the course of our development, the ego—originally an adaptive tool for survival—has become inflated. It began to interpret every experience through the narrow lens of self-preservation and self-importance, creating a gravitational pull that I have come to call "spiritual gravity." This misalignment of priorities not only distorts our perception but also sets us on a path of chronic suffering. It is here that GCT intervenes.

Gifted Compassionate Therapy does not seek to abolish the ego; rather, it aims to recalibrate it. The process begins with an honest, unflinching assessment of one's internal state. Clinicians who use this model are guided to measure the relative strength of the ego's influence versus the heart's guiding presence, identifying patterns where the ego's voice—often amplified by past traumas, societal conditioning, and self-limiting beliefs—overpowers the innate wisdom of the heart. In its unchecked form, the ego is like a tree that grows out of balance, its rings thickened by experiences of pain and misinterpretation. When the ego becomes the sole reference point, we are trapped in a cycle of reactivity and internal conflict. Our emotional wounds accumulate like blemishes on the rings, marking the passage of time with increasing suffering.

The algorithm of healing that GCT proposes is iterative and self-correcting. It begins with the initial input: an assessment of the individual's current state. This involves evaluating the magnitude of the ego (E) and the clarity of the heart as a guiding compass (Hc). In the dysfunctional, ego-solaristic state, suffering (S) is not a linear function but grows exponentially, as the ego's misinterpretations distort every experience. Mathematically, we express this state as $S = E^2 - Hc$. Here, even a modest increase in egoic dominance can lead to a disproportionate rise in suffering. On the other hand, when the heart is allowed to guide, and the ego is brought into a balanced, nominal state, suffering is recalibrated to $S = E + Hc$. In this natural state, the heart's influence tempers the ego, leading to a harmonious alignment that minimizes distress.

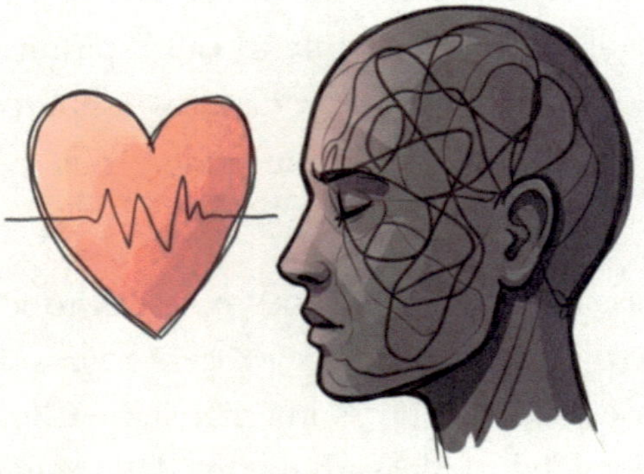

...the heart's influence tempers the ego's distress.

The process is not instantaneous; it requires mindful intervention and a willingness to engage in deep self-reflection. Techniques such as mindfulness meditation, narrative reframing, and compassionate inquiry serve as the therapeutic tools that gradually decrease the weight of ego-solarism. For instance, when a client experiences an emotionally charged event, they are encouraged to pause and activate their "Observer"—that part of the psyche that can witness without judgment. By creating a space for reflection, the client begins to recognize how the ego has colored their perception of the event. With the Observer's neutral insight, the client can then employ cognitive reframing to reinterpret the experience through the lens of the heart. This shift is akin to recalibrating a misaligned instrument; as the heart regains its central position, the overall state of suffering diminishes, and the individual begins to move toward a more balanced, authentic expression of self.

Integrating this algorithm into clinical practice involves a step-by-step process that mirrors the natural healing mechanisms inherent in both the body and the psyche. Initially, the therapist assists the client in identifying the presence and intensity of egoic distortions. This might involve exploring recurring narratives of self-criticism, unprocessed trauma, or a persistent need for external validation. Once these patterns are brought to light, the focus shifts to the heart's role. The client is guided to reconnect with the heart's wisdom through exercises that emphasize compassion, empathy, and mindfulness. Over time, as the client learns to regulate the ego by aligning it with the heart's compass, the therapeutic interventions become less about symptom management and more about fostering a deep, internal recalibration—a return to the natural state of homeostasis within the psyche.

The significance of this approach is profound. It challenges the conventional wisdom that equates a strong ego with a strong sense of self. Instead, it posits that true strength lies in the balance between the ego and the heart. When the ego dominates, suffering escalates; when the heart guides, suffering subsides, paving the way for what GCT calls "intentional evolution." This evolution is not merely about achieving a state of symptom-free existence; it is about embracing the full spectrum of human experience—acknowledging the pain, celebrating the growth, and ultimately moving toward a more compassionate and integrated way of living.

The integrated model of GCT, therefore, is both diagnostic and prescriptive. It provides a framework for understanding the root causes of suffering—misaligned perception, cognitive distortions, and the overemphasis on ego-driven narratives—and offers a pathway to transformation. The algorithm, $S = E^2 - Hc$ versus $S = E + Hc$, serves as a quantitative representation of this process, symbolizing the impact of internal balance on emotional well-being. It reminds us that the path to healing is not about extinguishing the ego altogether, but about realigning it with the heart's intrinsic wisdom.

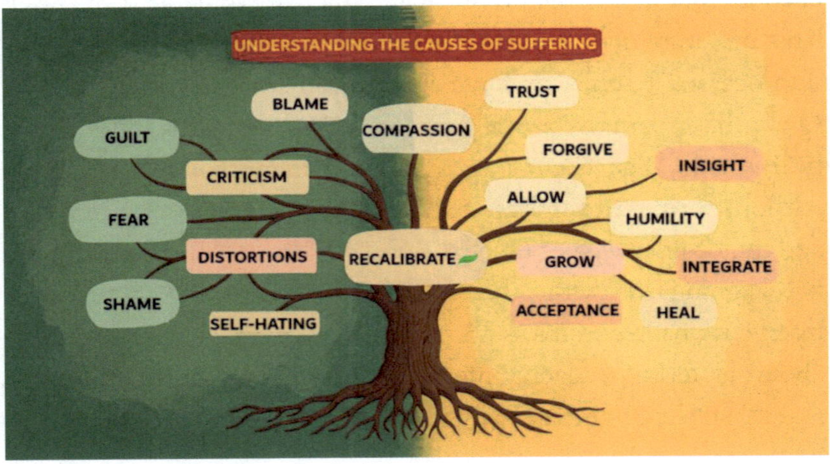


Throughout the therapeutic journey, the concept of the "humane spectrum" is introduced and becomes central. This spectrum represents the continuum between an existence dominated by egoic self-interest and one enriched by heart-centered compassion. It is the measure of how closely an individual aligns with life as intended—a state where truth is not distorted by the inflated self but illuminated by the clarity and warmth of the heart. For clinicians practicing GCT, the humane spectrum becomes a guidepost for assessing progress and tailoring interventions. It underscores the notion that every client has the innate capacity to self-correct, provided they can navigate past the false gravitational pull of ego-solarism.

As therapists, we must acknowledge the historical resistance to paradigm shifts—just as Galileo faced opposition for challenging the geocentric model, modern institutions often resist the idea that consciousness should be re-centered around the heart. Yet, history teaches us that truth, no matter how obscured by dogma or tradition, eventually emerges through persistent inquiry and courageous transformation. In our current era, where the pressures of modern life, societal disconnection, and technological manipulation compound the challenges of ego-solarism, the call for a heart-centered realignment has never been more urgent.

The transformation from ego-solarism to heart-centered awareness is, in essence, a call to reclaim our natural state of alignment—a state that has been obscured by the accumulated weight of misinterpretation, trauma, and conditioned responses. This process is iterative and ongoing; it requires both the humility to recognize our distortions and the courage to engage with our deepest wounds. As we gradually peel away the layers of egoic misinterpretation, we uncover the timeless truth that our inherent worth is not defined by external validation or societal labels, but by the quiet, steady guidance of the heart.

## Facilitating the Shift: Clinical Dialogue Examples

The transition from ego-solarism to heart-centered awareness is not merely theoretical—it requires skillful facilitation by the therapist through targeted interventions and carefully structured dialogue. The following examples demonstrate how clinicians can guide clients through this transformative process in actual therapeutic exchanges.

### Example 1: Activating the Observer with a Highly Self-Critical Client

**Context:** Sarah, a 42-year-old executive, enters therapy with intense self-criticism and perfectionism that have led to chronic anxiety and insomnia. Her critic lens dominates her internal dialogue.

**Therapist:** "I notice that when you talk about the presentation that didn't go as planned, your voice becomes tense and your breathing shallow. What's happening inside right now?"

**Client:** "I'm just so angry with myself. I should have been better prepared. Everyone probably thinks I'm incompetent now."

**Therapist:** "I'm wondering if we could try something. Could you take a moment to notice those thoughts as if you were witnessing them rather than being them? Almost as if you could step back and observe this critical voice with curiosity."

**Client:** "You mean like... watching myself think these thoughts?"

**Therapist:** "Exactly. As if there's a part of you that can notice the critic speaking, without immediately believing everything it says."

**Client:** *(after a pause)* "I can feel this harsh voice saying I'm a failure... but there's also something else... a quieter part that feels sad and exhausted from all this pressure."

**Therapist:** "That's the observer beginning to activate—that awareness that can witness the critic without being completely identified with it. What's it like to notice both the critic and this other perspective at the same time?"

**Client:** "It's strange... like I'm not just stuck inside the criticism anymore. There's a little space around it."

**Therapist:** "That space is crucial. It's the beginning of realizing that you are not your thoughts—you are the awareness that can notice them. How does your body feel as you maintain this observer perspective?"

**Client:** "My breathing feels less tight. My shoulders have dropped a bit."

**Therapist:** "This observer perspective is our starting point. From here, we can begin to understand how the critic lens developed to protect you, even as it causes suffering now. And more importantly, we can start to access the heart's wisdom, which offers a very different kind of guidance than the critic."

### Example 2: Reframing Through the Heart Lens with an Anxious Client

**Context:** Michael, a 35-year-old teacher, struggles with anticipatory anxiety about an upcoming evaluation. His mediator lens has kept him people-pleasing at work while internally experiencing mounting panic.

**Therapist:** "You've described all the things that might go wrong in this evaluation. I'm curious—if we could access a deeper wisdom within you, beyond the anxiety, what might that perspective offer?"

**Client:** "I don't know. The anxiety is all I can feel right now."

**Therapist:** "Let's try something. Place one hand on your heart area and take a few slow breaths. As you do this, imagine your heart as a center of wisdom and clarity." *(pauses while client follows instruction)* "Now, from this heart-centered awareness, what do you most need to remember about yourself as a teacher?"

**Client:** *(after a pause, voice softening)* "That I do this because I care about my students. That even when I make mistakes, my intention is to help them grow."

**Therapist:** "Notice how different that feels from the anxious thoughts. That's your heart lens offering a more compassionate, centered perspective. How does your body respond to this view compared to the anxiety?"

**Client:** "It feels... warmer. More grounded. Like I'm reconnecting with why I became a teacher in the first place."

**Therapist:** "This is a crucial distinction in our work together. The mediator lens that tries to please everyone comes from a place of fear—fear of conflict, fear of disapproval. But the heart lens accesses your authentic values and purpose. When decisions come from this place, they're guided by clarity rather than fear."

**Client:** "So when I feel that anxiety rising, I can try to shift to this heart perspective?"

**Therapist:** "Exactly. Not to deny the anxiety, but to create space around it by first activating your observer, and then gently shifting to the heart's guidance. This isn't about forcing positive thinking—

it's about accessing a more integrated wisdom that lies beyond the ego's reactivity."

**Example 3: Addressing Spiritual Gravity with a Trauma Survivor**

**Context:** Elena, a 29-year-old trauma survivor, describes feeling "heavy" and "weighted down" by her experiences. Her bully lens manifests as aggressive self-protection and difficulty with vulnerability in relationships.

**Therapist:** "You've mentioned several times that you feel 'heavy' or 'weighed down.' I'm wondering if we could explore that sensation as a form of what I call 'spiritual gravity'—a weight that comes from carrying the ego's distortions."

**Client:** "What do you mean?"

**Therapist:** "When we experience trauma, the ego often takes on a protective role—in your case, the bully lens that keeps others at a distance to prevent further hurt. This was necessary for survival then, but now it's creating a weight that isn't actually yours to carry."

**Client:** "It does feel like I'm always bracing for attack. Like I can never relax."

**Therapist:** "Let's try to locate that weight in your body. Where do you feel it most intensely?"

**Client:** "In my chest and shoulders. Like I'm carrying something heavy."

**Therapist:** "As you notice that sensation, can you also recognize that there's a part of you—your observer—that can witness this weight without being crushed by it? This observer has always been there, even during your most difficult moments."

**Client:** *(after focusing)* "Yes... it's like there's the heaviness, but also something else that's... watching the heaviness."

**Therapist:** "That's it. Now, from this observer perspective, I'd like you to gently place your attention on your heart area. Beyond the protective armor, there's a natural wisdom here that knows you deserve connection and peace. Can you sense any glimpse of that?"

**Client:** *(tearing up)* "There's something there... a feeling that maybe I don't have to fight so hard all the time. That maybe it's safe to put some of this down."

**Therapist:** "That recognition is profound. The weight you feel isn't your natural state—it's the accumulated effect of the ego's protective strategies. As we continue our work together, we'll help you distinguish between what's truly yours to carry and what can be released as you realign with your heart's guidance."

**Client:** "It feels like taking off a heavy backpack I didn't even know I was wearing."

**Therapist:** "That's exactly what the release of spiritual gravity feels like. Not a rejection of your experiences, but a reframing that allows you to carry them differently—with the heart's compassion rather than the ego's vigilance."

---

These dialogues illustrate how therapists can facilitate the shift from ego-solarism to heart-centered awareness through specific verbal interventions. The key elements include:

1. **Noticing and naming** ego patterns as they arise in session
2. **Activating the observer** through mindful awareness
3. **Physically orienting** to the heart center

4. **Distinguishing between** ego-driven and heart-centered perspectives
5. **Validating the protective function** of ego patterns while introducing alternatives
6. **Tracking somatic shifts** as clients move between different states of alignment

Through these targeted interventions, therapists help clients experience—rather than merely understand intellectually—the difference between ego-driven suffering and heart-centered clarity. This experiential dimension is essential for true transformation and intentional evolution.

In practice, the implementation of the healing algorithm within GCT involves a range of therapeutic modalities. Mindfulness and meditation practices help activate the Observer, allowing clients to witness their internal experiences without judgment. Narrative reframing techniques encourage clients to reinterpret their life stories in a way that emphasizes resilience and growth rather than victimhood. Compassion-focused therapy methods guide clients to cultivate a deeper, more empathetic relationship with themselves, thereby diminishing the reactive force of an overactive ego. Over time, these interventions work synergistically to reduce the exponential impact of ego-solarism, moving clients toward a state of balanced, heart-centered consciousness.

Ultimately, the algorithm of intentional evolution encapsulated by the equations $E^2 - Hc = \uparrow S$ and $E + Hc = \downarrow S$ is a clarion call for a new way of being. It asserts that the true center of our existence is not the ego—the inflated, reactive part that clings to a distorted self-image—but the heart, the wellspring of compassion, clarity, and connection. When we allow the heart to guide us, we unlock our innate capacity for healing and growth, creating a life that is not defined by suffering but by intentional, purposeful evolution.

The challenge for contemporary therapists is to help clients navigate this internal shift, to guide them in recognizing that every moment of pain is also a moment of potential transformation. In doing so, we not only alleviate individual suffering but also contribute to a broader cultural evolution—a movement away from the isolation and disconnection of ego-solarism toward a more integrated, compassionate way of living. As professionals dedicated to holistic and integrative healing, we stand at the threshold of a new paradigm. The journey is arduous, the stakes high, and the resistance formidable, but the promise of intentional evolution—a reawakening of the heart as our true compass—offers a path forward that is as inspiring as it is necessary.

In closing, this chapter is both a theoretical exposition and a practical guide. It invites therapists to embrace a model of healing that honors the complexity of the human experience. It calls on us to see the ego not as the enemy but as a misunderstood adaptive function, one that can be recalibrated through the deliberate, compassionate interventions of GCT. By integrating the algorithm of intentional evolution into our practice, we have the opportunity to transform not only the lives of our clients but the very fabric of our society. The shift from ego-solarism to heart-centered alignment is not a distant dream—it is an achievable reality that begins with a single, courageous step: the decision to let the heart lead.

As we conclude our exploration of the journey from ego-solarism to heart-centered healing, we have established the fundamental algorithm that governs intentional evolution: when the ego is exaggerated and the heart's guidance diminished ($E^2 - Hc = \uparrow S$), suffering increases; conversely, when the ego functions in balanced partnership with the heart ($E + Hc = \downarrow S$), suffering naturally decreases. This algorithm is not merely theoretical—it represents the measurable dynamics of alignment that we observe in clinical practice.

With this foundation in place, we now turn our attention to the specific components that comprise the GCT framework. Chapter Four will deepen our understanding of ego-solarism, the alignment equation, and the five lenses of perception—providing the detailed architecture through which intentional evolution operates. These foundational concepts serve as the practical building blocks that enable therapists to systematically assess misalignment and guide clients toward authentic, heart-centered living.

As we move forward, consider how each component contributes to the larger healing algorithm we have established, and how these elements might manifest in your own clinical work. The conceptual framework that follows offers not just theory, but actionable insights that transform suffering into opportunities for growth and alignment.

# Chapter Four
# Foundational Concepts of GCT

In the previous chapter, we explored the philosophy of intentional evolution, which frames the human psyche as a self-correcting system designed to return to its natural state of alignment. This philosophy forms the cornerstone of Gifted Compassionate Therapy (GCT), asserting that healing is not about "fixing" brokenness but about realigning with the heart as the guiding compass and honoring the psyche's innate capacity for restoration (Vecchio, 2025). In this chapter, we build upon that foundation by delving deeply into the core components of GCT and outlining the comprehensive framework that directs its application. Our exploration will not only describe each element but also interweave their dynamic interplay to underscore how they collectively foster a process of intentional evolution—a process that emphasizes balance, clarity, and compassionate self-inquiry.

## The Core Components of GCT

At the heart of GCT lies a nuanced conceptualization of the human psyche. Rather than viewing psychological components as isolated elements, GCT integrates four interdependent facets that work together to navigate life's challenges and facilitate internal alignment. These components are described below in detail:

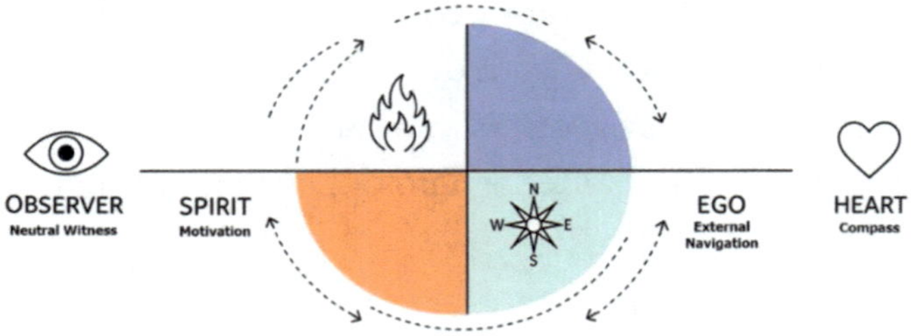

**The Observer:**
The Observer is the part of the psyche that witnesses life's events without judgment. It serves as a neutral, higher level of consciousness, allowing individuals to step back and view their thoughts, emotions, and behaviors from a detached perspective. This detachment is crucial because it prevents reactive patterns from overwhelming our ability to perceive reality accurately. In clinical practice, cultivating the Observer is akin to mindfulness techniques that help clients achieve a state of non-reactivity, thereby enabling clearer insight into their internal processes (Siegel, 2012). Observing shifts from 'who' is looking to 'what' is fully seeing.

**The Spirit:**
The Spirit represents the energetic, emotional, and experiential facet of the self. It is the motivator and provocateur—fueling creativity, passion, and growth, while also sometimes provoking discomfort when unresolved wounds surface. In therapy, acknowledging the spirit's role is essential because it connects clients to their emotional truth. The spirit's impulses, if unrecognized, may lead to dysregulation; however, when integrated with awareness, they can be powerful drivers for healing and transformation.

**The Ego:**
The Ego functions as the adaptive tool that helps us navigate external realities. It is responsible for constructing our sense of identity and is necessary for functioning in everyday life. However, when the ego becomes overly dominant, it distorts perception by amplifying reactive and defensive patterns. Clinically, this overactive ego can manifest as excessive self-criticism or rigid control strategies. While it is an important

protective mechanism, the ego must remain in balance to prevent the creation of internal suffering.

**The Heart:**
The Heart is the true compass of the psyche. It anchors alignment by integrating emotional, cognitive, and intuitive insights. When the heart leads, decisions are made from a place of authenticity and compassion. The heart's function in GCT is to guide individuals back to their natural state—a state in which clarity and emotional regulation are restored. Research on heart coherence (McCraty et al., 2015) supports the idea that the heart, with its powerful electromagnetic field, plays a central role in harmonizing physiological and psychological processes.

Each of these components plays a distinct yet interrelated role in the psyche's functioning. Their dynamic interplay forms the basis for understanding how misalignment can lead to suffering—and, conversely, how intentional rebalancing can foster healing.

## What Distinguishes GCT from Traditional Models

Many traditional therapeutic approaches tend to focus on managing symptoms through compartmentalization, isolating specific behaviors or emotional responses for treatment. In contrast, GCT adopts a holistic framework that addresses the entire psyche. It views suffering not as a flaw to be eradicated but as a signal that invites the individual to reconnect with their authentic, heart-guided self. This approach is built on several distinguishing pillars:

**A Holistic Approach:**
GCT attends to the entirety of the psyche by recognizing the integral roles of the observer, spirit, ego, and heart. Instead of isolating symptoms, GCT aims to restore balance across the system. This integrated method is reflective of contemporary

trends in trauma psychology that emphasize the mind–body connection (van der Kolk, 2014).

**A Self-Corrective Focus:**
Rather than positioning clients as passive recipients of therapeutic interventions, GCT empowers them to harness their innate capacity for realignment and growth. This empowerment is achieved through cultivating internal resources such as mindfulness, self-awareness, and emotional regulation—processes that ultimately reduce suffering.

**Practical Accessibility:**
GCT offers a framework that is not only theoretically robust but also practically applicable. Clients are provided with intuitive tools and techniques that resonate with everyday experiences. These tools are designed to facilitate a shift from reactive, ego-driven patterns to a state of intentional alignment, thereby making the therapeutic process both accessible and transformative (Vecchio, 2025).

## Chapter Goals and Structure

In this chapter, our objectives are multifold. We will:

**Define and Explore the Core Components:**
We will detail the unique functions of the observer, spirit, ego, and heart, examining how each contributes to the process of alignment and intentional evolution.

**Understand the Dynamics of Interplay:**
We will investigate how misalignment occurs when these components are in conflict and how GCT's interventions work to re-center the heart's role, thereby restoring balance.

**Apply Concepts to Real-World Challenges:**
Through practical examples and case studies, we will illustrate how these foundational ideas are applied in therapeutic contexts, highlighting their relevance in navigating suffering, decision-making, and relationship challenges.

Additionally, throughout the chapter, supplementary discussions will integrate broader theoretical contexts and additional references to support our framework. This ensures that while the narrative remains accessible, it is also grounded in rigorous clinical and academic insights.

## A Roadmap for Growth and Healing

The foundational concepts of GCT provide a clear roadmap for navigating the inner landscape with intentionality, clarity, and compassion. By understanding and integrating the roles of the observer, spirit, ego, and heart, individuals can embark on a transformative journey that reduces suffering and fosters genuine growth. This roadmap encourages:

**Reduction of Suffering Through Alignment:**
By addressing internal misalignments and integrating the disparate components of the psyche, individuals learn to process life's challenges with greater balance. Rather than suppressing pain or resorting to reactive patterns, they engage in a process that gradually diminishes suffering.

**Cultivation of Self-Awareness and Emotional Clarity:**
Engaging with the observer and heart fosters heightened awareness of internal states, allowing individuals to distinguish between immediate emotional responses and long-held narratives that no longer serve them.

**Intentional Engagement With Growth and Healing:**
The process of alignment is not passive. It involves deliberate self-reflection, a willingness to confront difficult emotions, and the courage to integrate fragmented parts of the self. In doing so, individuals move toward a more humane and resilient existence.

By integrating these elements, GCT lays out a comprehensive pathway that not only alleviates distress but also promotes an enduring sense of purpose and connection.

## 3.1 Ego Solarism: A False Centering of the Ego

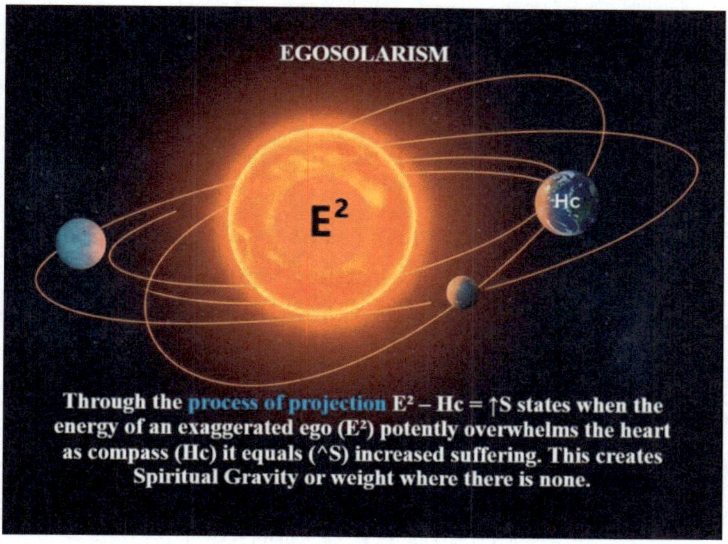


Ego solarism is the phenomenon in which the ego assumes a central, all-encompassing role within the psyche, creating an illusory sense of control and self-sufficiency. Much like the archaic belief in an Earth-centered universe, ego solarism positions the ego as the focal point of human experience. This false centering obscures the role of the heart—the true compass—and disrupts the natural process of alignment (Vecchio, 2025).

### Elaborating on the Dynamics of Ego Solarism

Although the ego is essential for adapting to external realities, it was never intended to dictate internal truth. Cultural narratives often reinforce the dominance of the ego by glorifying competition, achievement, and external validation as primary markers of success. Under such influences, the ego evolves into a self-perpetuating system that convinces itself—and the individual—that it alone can resolve the complexities of life. This belief not only isolates the individual from the heart's intuitive wisdom but also sets the stage for chronic misalignment.

**Practical Manifestations of Ego Solarism**

Ego solarism is not an abstract idea but is evident in everyday behaviors and thought patterns. For example, consider the following manifestations:

**Overthinking:**
The ego produces an incessant stream of analysis that can lead to confusion rather than clarity. In therapeutic settings, clients may report feeling trapped in loops of rumination, where every thought is scrutinized to the point of paralysis.

**Self-Criticism:**
Operating through what I call the critic lens; the ego magnifies feelings of shame and guilt. Every mistake becomes evidence of personal failure, reinforcing negative self-beliefs.

**Excessive Control:**
When functioning through the bully lens, the ego seeks to dominate external circumstances. This overcontrol is often a defense mechanism—a way to mask deep-seated fears of vulnerability.

Each of these patterns reinforces the illusion of an all-powerful ego, thereby disconnecting the individual from the heart's clarity and compassion. Such distortions are at the core of spiritual and emotional suffering.

## Spiritual Gravity: The False Weight of the Ego

Accompanying the concept of ego solarism is the condition it creates—spiritual gravity. Spiritual gravity is the artificial weight imposed on the psyche by an overactive and exaggerated ego. Analogous to physical gravity—which pulls objects toward a central mass—spiritual gravity creates a force that drags the individual away from alignment. However, unlike physical gravity, this weight is illusory; it is maintained solely by the ego's fixation on control and dominance.

This false weight manifests in several ways:

**Resistance to Change:**
The inertia of spiritual gravity makes it difficult to break free from entrenched egoic patterns, even when those patterns no longer serve the individual's well-being.

**Emotional Inertia:**
Emotions such as fear, shame, and anger are amplified under the influence of spiritual gravity, leading to recurring cycles of reactivity.

**Disconnection from the Heart:**
As the ego's dominance intensifies, the heart's role as the true compass becomes increasingly obscured, limiting access to compassionate insight.

In clinical practice, addressing spiritual gravity is key. It involves recognizing that the weight felt is not an inherent truth but rather a distortion created by the overemphasis on ego. As mentioned earlier, the following equation encapsulates this dynamic:

$$E^2 - Hc = \uparrow S$$

(Exaggerated Ego – Heart as Compass = Increased Suffering)

### The Role of GCT in Restoring Balance

Gifted Compassionate Therapy offers a structured framework for dismantling the illusions created by ego solarism and the weight of spiritual gravity. The therapeutic process focuses on rebalancing the psyche by engaging all four components:

**Recognizing Ego Solarism:**
Clients are guided to identify the specific egoic patterns—such as over analysis, self-blame, or a compulsive need for control—that lead to disconnection and suffering.

**Reducing Spiritual Gravity:**
Through targeted interventions, GCT helps clients release the false weight of an overactive ego. Techniques might include mindfulness, somatic experiencing, and narrative reframing, all aimed at reducing the inertia that holds the individual back.

**Restoring the Heart as Compass:**
The ultimate goal of GCT is to reinstate the heart as the central guide. When the heart leads, decisions are informed by clarity and compassion rather than fear or control. The re-establishment of the heart's central role is expressed by the following equation:

$$E + Hc = \downarrow S$$

(Nominal Ego + Heart as Compass = Decreased Suffering)

A practical example illustrates this process well. Consider a client who struggles with the need for overcontrol in personal and professional relationships. Her ego, functioning predominantly through the bully lens, convinces her that rigid control will prevent failure and ensure success. However, this very need for control alienates her from authentic connection, leaving her feeling isolated. In therapy, she learns to activate her Observer, gaining insight into the underlying fear driving her behavior. With gentle guidance, she reconnects with her heart, beginning to trust in its compassionate wisdom. Over time, as the false weight of spiritual gravity diminishes, she experiences alignment—a state marked by clarity, emotional freedom, and reduced suffering.

## Conclusion

Ego solarism and the resulting spiritual gravity represent fundamental distortions within the psyche. By centering the ego and magnifying its influence, these forces not only perpetuate suffering but also disconnect individuals from their natural capacity for healing. Gifted Compassionate Therapy addresses these distortions directly, offering pathways to dismantle them and reestablish the heart as the primary compass. In doing so, GCT enables individuals to transcend the illusions of ego dominance and rediscover life as it was intended: lived with clarity, connection, and compassion (Vecchio, 2025).

## 3.2 The Alignment Equation

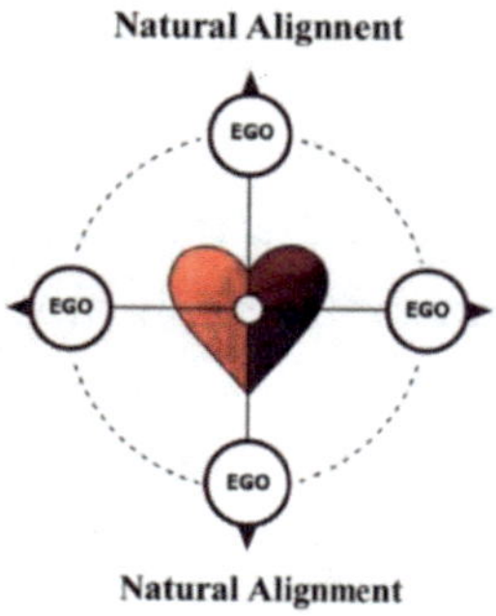

**Revisiting the Equation for Alignment**

At the core of GCT lies a simple yet profound equation that encapsulates the natural state of the psyche:

This equation describes an inner universe of human consciousness and experience. It states that when the energy of an exaggerated ego ($E^2$) potently overwhelms the heart as compass (Hc) it equals (^S) increased suffering. It highlights the deep relationship between ego and heart which is fundamental to understanding how people navigate their emotional landscape. We know this as 'life as it is.' This imbalance is expressed as follows:

$$\mathbf{E + Hc = \downarrow S}$$

In contrast, 'life as intended' is (Nominal Ego + Heart as Compass = Decreased Suffering). This equation suggests that when the ego operates in a balanced, supportive role and the heart leads with clarity and compassion, the result is a marked decrease in suffering. This balance is expressed as follows:

$$\mathbf{E^2 - Hc = \uparrow S}$$

**Deepening Our Understanding**

Alignment is not something to be achieved externally—it is a natural state that emerges when the inner components of the psyche are in harmony. The heart's electromagnetic field, which research has shown to be considerably more potent than that of the brain (McCraty et al., 2015), symbolizes its critical role in providing intuitive and emotional clarity. However, an exaggerated ego can disrupt this balance, initiating cycles of resistance, emotional reactivity, and suffering.

## The Impact of Spiritual Gravity on the Soul-Spirit-Ego-Heart System

Spiritual gravity—the weight imposed by over dominant egoic distortions—affects the interplay between the soul, spirit, ego, and heart. This concept is enriched by understanding the following:

**The Illusion of Weight and the Ego:**
The ego is particularly vulnerable to the pull of spiritual gravity because it interprets life through adaptive yet fear-based lenses. For instance, the critic lens may constantly assert, "I'm not enough; I must do more," while the bully lens might insist, "I must control to protect myself." These narratives create a false sense of weight that manifests guilt, shame, or fear, distancing the individual from the heart's clarity.

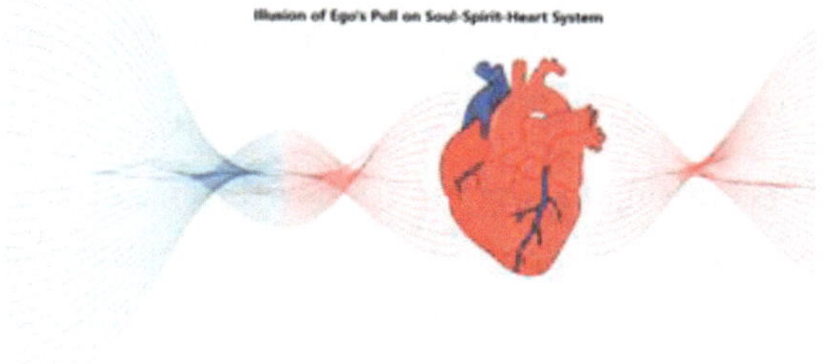


**The Spirit: Experiencing the Weight:**
The spirit, as the repository of emotional experience, directly absorbs the burden of spiritual gravity. This may appear as a persistent sense of heaviness or as recurring cycles of unresolved emotions that block authentic engagement with life. The spirit's natural lightness and flow become stifled when overwhelmed by the ego's distortions.

**The Soul: A Neutral Witness:**
In contrast, the soul remains unburdened by spiritual gravity. It functions as a neutral observer, perceiving the distortions without being drawn into them. However, when the ego or spirit is overactive, the pathway to the soul's neutral perspective may be obstructed, making it more challenging to access the clarity and wisdom it offers. The observer's preferred lens of perception is the heart NOT the ego.

**Restoring Balance in the System**

To counter the distorting effects of spiritual gravity, the system must be realigned:

- The **soul** must observe without judgment.
- The **heart** must resume its role as the primary guide.
- The **ego** must release its overblown sense of responsibility.
- The **spirit** must reconnect with the heart's compassion and the soul's neutrality.

Practical interventions in therapy focus on these areas. Techniques such as mindfulness, guided imagery, and reflective journaling can help clients develop an awareness of this internal interplay, gradually releasing the false weight of spiritual gravity.

**The Heart as Compass: Countering Spiritual Gravity**

The heart serves as the guiding force of the psyche, offering insights based on authenticity, compassion, and connection. In moments when spiritual gravity exerts its influence, the heart reminds the individual that the weight is an illusion. For example, a gentle internal prompt such as "Let go of this burden" may be countered by the ego's insistence on maintaining control. However, when the heart's perspective prevails, the individual is led toward a state of lightness and balance, where reactive emotions are replaced by clarity and reciprocal connection.

**Practical Steps to Counter Spiritual Gravity**

To translate this theoretical framework into practical change, GCT outlines the following steps:

**Awareness (Soul):**
Cultivate a clear recognition that the heavy sensations experienced are not inherent truths, but distortions created by an overactive ego.

**Compassion (Heart):**
Embrace self-compassion, allowing the heart to guide responses to emotional distress. Suffer 'with' the self and heal versus suffer 'for' the self as victim.

**Integration (Spirit):**
Reconnect with present-moment experiences and allow the spirit to experience freedom and lightness.

**Adaptation (Ego):**
Gradually reframe limiting beliefs and replace the need for control with trust in the heart's wisdom.

**Conclusion**

The alignment equation is a central tenet of GCT that illustrates the delicate balance between the ego and the heart. By acknowledging the distortions brought about by spiritual gravity and actively working to restore balance, individuals can realign their internal systems, reducing suffering and fostering a state of natural harmony. This process is at the core of what it means to live authentically and with compassionate intentionality (McCraty et al., 2015; Vecchio, 2025).

## 3.3 Understanding Ego Solarism as States of Being

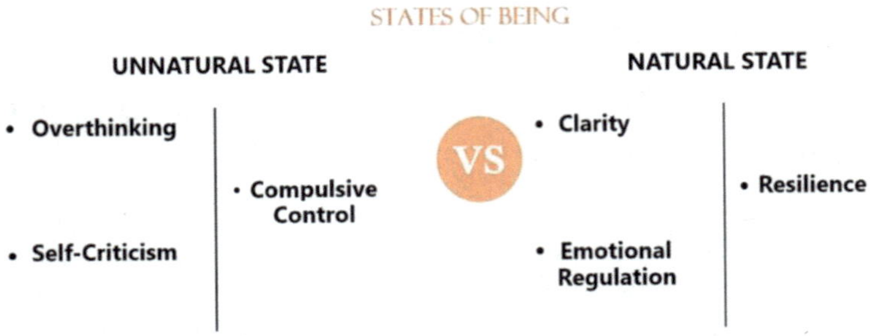


In the realm of the human psyche, the ego is indispensable for navigating external challenges and forming our sense of identity. However, when the ego becomes overly dominant—a phenomenon I call ego solarism—it distorts our natural alignment. This section examines ego solarism through the lens of two distinct states of being:

**The Unnatural State:**
Characterized by exaggerated ego dominance, this state is marked by chronic emotional suffering, resistance, and a pervasive sense of disconnection. In this condition, the ego's overactivity is captured by the equation:

$$\mathbf{E^2 - Hc = \uparrow S}$$

(Exaggerated Ego – Heart as Compass = Increased Suffering). Here, the individual experiences overthinking, heightened self-criticism, and a compulsive need for control. For example, a client might find that every setback reinforces an internal narrative of inadequacy, leading to persistent self-doubt and shame. This state is reinforced by cultural narratives that glorify achievement and external validation, leaving little room for vulnerability.

**The Natural State:**
In contrast, the natural state emerges when the heart takes precedence, allowing the ego to serve in a supportive role rather than a controlling one. Expressed by the equation:

$$\mathbf{E + Hc = \downarrow S}$$

(Nominal Ego + Heart as Compass = Decreased Suffering),this state is characterized by clarity, emotional regulation, and resilience. In the natural state, individuals process challenges with a sense of openness and authenticity. For example, a person facing career uncertainty might engage in reflective practices that reveal hidden strengths and a deep inner sense of purpose, leading to balanced decision-making and a reduction in reactive distress.

## How GCT Reveals Alignment

Gifted Compassionate Therapy offers a transformative pathway to move from the unnatural to the natural state. Key interventions include:

**Activating the Observer:**
Clients learn to adopt a neutral, mindful stance that views ego distortions as informative signals rather than intrinsic flaws (Rogers, 1961). This activation is critical in allowing them to step back from reactive patterns.

**Reconnecting with the Heart:**
Therapeutic practices such as guided imagery, meditative reflection, and embodied exercises help clients rediscover the heart's role as the true compass.

**Balancing the Ego:**
Through narrative therapy and cognitive reframing, clients learn to adjust the ego's role, recalibrating it so that it supports the heart's direction rather than overriding it (Vecchio, 2025).

*Case Study: Sarah's Journey to Alignment*

Consider Sarah, a client whose life has been dominated by an exaggerated ego. Her need for control, particularly in interpersonal relationships, often manifests as overbearing behavior and emotional isolation. In therapy, Sarah learns to identify the bully lens—a manifestation of her overactive ego—through which she externalizes blame and seeks to dominate her environment. With the guidance of GCT techniques, she begins to activate her Observer, recognizing that her need for control is rooted in deep-seated fears of vulnerability. Over time, as she reconnects with her heart and learns to trust its guidance, Sarah transitions from an unnatural state of isolation to a natural state characterized by authentic connection and reduced suffering.

**Conclusion**

Understanding ego solarism as states of being provides a clear framework for recognizing and addressing the distortions that lead to chronic suffering. By distinguishing between the unnatural state (dominated by an exaggerated ego) and the natural state (guided by the heart), GCT empowers individuals to reclaim their innate capacity for clarity, compassion, and authentic self-expression (McCraty et al., 2015; Rogers, 1961; Vecchio, 2025).

## 3.4 The Five Lenses of Perception

### Introduction to the Lenses

The human psyche navigates experience through a series of perceptual filters, which GCT conceptualizes as five primary lenses. Four of these are egoic lenses—the critic, bully, mediator, and counselor—while the fifth is the heart lens. Each lens shapes how experiences are interpreted, influencing thoughts, emotions, and behaviors. Although the egoic lenses serve as adaptive tools under certain conditions, their prolonged dominance can distort perception, leading to misalignment and increased suffering. In contrast, the heart lens emerges when the ego relinquishes control, allowing clarity, compassion, and authentic connection to come to the fore (Vecchio, 2025).

### The Four Egoic Lenses

*Function:* The critic lens zeroes in on perceived flaws and shortcomings.

*Distortion:* Overuse leads to pervasive self-doubt, shame, and perfectionism.

*Example:* A client might internalize every mistake as a sign of personal failure, reinforcing a cycle of negative self-talk.

*Function:* The bully lens externalizes blame and reacts with aggression or defensiveness when faced with threats.

*Distortion:* This lens often masks vulnerability with hostility, reinforcing conflict and isolation.

*Example:* An individual may lash out during stressful situations as a way to assert control, thereby straining relationships.

**MEDIATOR LENS**

*Function:* The mediator lens seeks compromise and harmony, often prioritizing peace over authentic expression.

*Distortion:* Its overreliance can lead to avoidance of genuine emotional expression and internal conflict.

*Example:* A person might consistently suppress personal needs to maintain external harmony, resulting in unacknowledged resentment.

*Function:* The counselor lens offers guidance, self-reflection, and problem-solving perspectives.

*Distortion:* When overly relied upon, it may result in intellectualizing emotions and avoiding direct emotional engagement.

*Example:* A client might analyze their feelings excessively, which hinders the natural processing of emotions.

*Function:* The heart lens is the preference of our neutral observer, offering us an ethical and contextual view of the whole of our lives.

*Distortion:* When used as an afterthought by the ego, it will be contaminated or blocked by emotions; this means present-tense feelings are secondary.

*Example:* A person may know deeply what is true, but the ego will overwhelm their feelings and cause them to focus on simply what's right or wrong.

### The Heart Lens: The Preferred Perspective

The heart lens represents the integration of emotional, cognitive, and intuitive insights. It emerges naturally when the ego's influence is tempered by humility and self-compassion. Characteristics of the heart lens include:

**Allowing, Not Forcing:**
The heart lens unfolds naturally when the ego steps aside rather than imposing its agenda.

**Humility as the Gateway:**
The experiences that humble the ego pave the way for the heart's wisdom to emerge.

**Outcome:**
When the heart lens leads, perception shifts from distortion to clarity and alignment, which in turn reduces suffering and fosters resilience.

*The Spirit as Provoker and Motivator*
The spirit plays a dual role in perception:

*Provoker:*
When the ego dominates, the spirit amplifies discomfort, signaling the need for transformation. This provocation serves as a wake-up call, urging the individual to

examine their maladaptive patterns. *Motivator:* When the heart is in the lead, the spirit inspires forward momentum—energizing the individual to embrace authentic, heart-led actions (Van der Kolk, 2014).

**When the heart is in the lead, the spirit inspires forward momentum—energizing the individual to embrace authentic, heart-led actions (Van der Kolk, 2014).**

### The Observer's Role in Lens Recognition

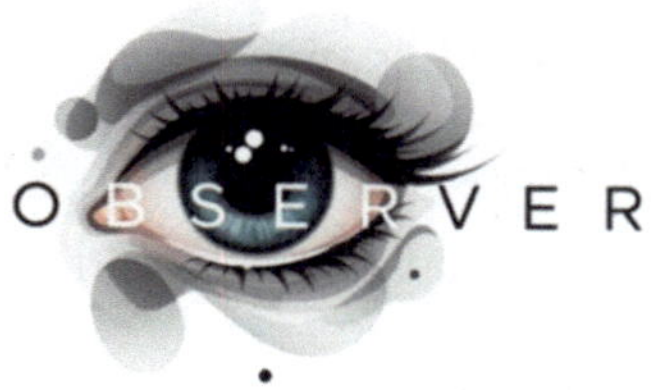


The Observer is the impartial witness within the psyche. Its function is not to choose a lens but to recognize which lens is active at any given moment. By creating a space of nonjudgmental awareness, the Observer helps to:

**Facilitate Allowance:**
Identify when the ego's dominance distorts perception.

**Enable Humility:**
Foster the humility necessary for the ego to yield, thereby allowing the heart to guide perception.

### Salt and Oil: The Byproducts of Transformation

The metaphors of salt and oil capture the transformative potential of suffering when processed with humility and self-compassion:

**Salt as Wisdom:**
The insights gained from life's challenges serve as enduring lessons for growth.

**Oil as Healing Essence:**
Self-compassion acts as an emotional lubricant, reducing friction between the ego and the spirit, thus enabling the heart to emerge as the primary guide.

For example, an individual processing deep-seated shame might eventually recognize that the pain has led to a greater capacity for empathy and understanding (salt), while practicing self-compassion helps ease the tension that once kept them stuck in reactive patterns (oil).

**Practical Application in Therapy**

In practical therapeutic settings, understanding the five lenses offers clients a framework for self-exploration:

**Identifying the Active Lens:**
Clients learn to observe which lens is currently coloring their perception.

**Activating the Observer:**
Through mindfulness, journaling, and guided reflection, clients develop the capacity to witness their experiences without judgment.

**Engaging the Heart Lens:**
By practicing humility and self-compassion, clients allow the heart's clarity to emerge, transforming suffering into wisdom and healing.

**Conclusion**

The interplay among the five lenses—the four egoic lenses and the heart lens—plays a critical role in how individuals interpret and navigate their experiences. While egoic lenses may distort perception when left unchecked, the heart lens provides the clarity, compassion, and alignment necessary for genuine healing. Gifted Compassionate Therapy leverages this understanding to help clients move beyond ego solarism, rediscovering their innate capacity for resilience, authenticity, and humane connection.

### 3.5 Answering Life's Five Big Questions Through Alignment

Human beings are natural seekers, driven by the desire to explore fundamental questions of identity, purpose, and connection. Gifted Compassionate Therapy identifies five existential questions as pivotal guideposts for this journey: **When am I? Where am I? Who am I? What am I? Why am I?** These questions are not abstract musings but practical tools for navigating suffering, reclaiming alignment, and engaging in intentional evolution (Vecchio, 2025).

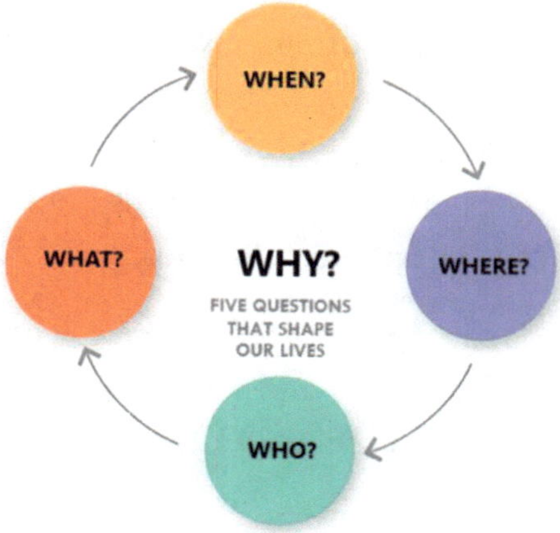


### Exploring the Five Questions and Their GCT Insights

#### When am I?

*Insight:* This question distinguishes between being fully present in the moment and being caught in past-oriented emotional narratives. It invites clients to differentiate between immediate feelings and the overlay of historical emotional patterns.

*In Practice:* Consider Mary, who experiences overwhelming guilt whenever she sets healthy boundaries, a guilt rooted in childhood beliefs that self-care is selfish. By learning to distinguish her present feelings from those entrenched narratives, Mary begins to respond more authentically, free from reactive loops.

*GCT Insight:* Stepping out of these reactive loops allows individuals to engage with the present moment more fully, thereby reducing suffering and fostering a natural flow of life (Vecchio, 2025).

**Where am I?**

*Insight:* This question invites clients to explore both their external positioning and internal emotional truth. It challenges them to locate themselves in the present moment by accessing the heart's guidance for emotional grounding.

*In Practice:* John, a high-performing executive, despite his external success, feels profoundly lost. In therapy, he learns to *close his eyes and "look' with something else--the heart.* In this moment, he discovers that his sense of disconnection stems not from external circumstances but from an internal avoidance of vulnerability.

*GCT Insight:* Reconnecting with one's internal state bridges the gap between external distractions and inner clarity, fostering a more grounded sense of self (Vecchio, 2025).

**Who am I?**

*Insight:* This question differentiates between the adaptive roles constructed by the ego and the deeper, authentic self that emerges when the heart is allowed to guide perception.

*In Practice:* Karen, a devoted caregiver, defines herself solely through her role as a mother. When her children leave home, she feels untethered and questions her identity. Through therapy, she discovers that her identity is multifaceted—encompassing creativity, connection, and authenticity that go beyond any single role.

*GCT Insight:* Recognizing that ego-based roles are transient enables the deeper, more integrated self to emerge (Rogers, 1961).

**What am I?**

*Insight:* This question invites exploration of the essence of human consciousness—beyond labels and roles, seeking the unifying, observing self that exists prior to ego formation. Life changes when we give station to 'what' is looking instead of who.

*In Practice:* Lisa, a trauma survivor, struggles to define herself without referencing her pain. GCT guides her to reconnect with her pre-ego essence—a resilient core that persists beyond her suffering, allowing her to reclaim a sense of wholeness.

*GCT Insight:* Rediscovering the essence of being shifts the focus from survival to intentional evolution, revealing the unbroken, intelligent core that underlies the ego (Vecchio, 2025).

**Why am I?**

*Insight:* This question moves beyond the ego's pursuit of external validation to the heart's search for purpose and reciprocal connection with life. It challenges the individual to find meaning that transcends mere survival.

*In Practice:* Jacob, a retired teacher, feels aimless after leaving his career. In therapy, he discovers that his purpose lies in mentoring and community engagement—a realization that reconnects him with a sense of fulfillment and mutual contribution.

*GCT Insight:* Aligning with life's intended flow through authentic contribution fosters a deeper sense of purpose that goes beyond egoic concerns (McCraty et al., 2015).

### The GCT Distinction: Focusing on What and Why

While many individuals become entangled in the ego-driven questions of Who, When, and Where—thus anchoring themselves to reactive patterns—GCT emphasizes the importance of the heart-driven questions: What and Why. The former invite an exploration of one's essence, while the latter open the door to a purpose rooted in authenticity and reciprocal connection. By guiding clients to engage with these deeper inquiries, GCT facilitates a transformative shift from symptom management to profound personal evolution.

### Conclusion

Answering life's five big questions is far more than an intellectual exercise. It is a transformative journey that enables individuals to transcend egoic distortions, reconnect with their authentic selves, and align with a life marked by clarity, purpose, and compassionate connection (Vecchio, 2025). This process, facilitated through the lens of Gifted Compassionate Therapy, helps individuals reclaim their innate capacity for intentional evolution—a journey from suffering toward a life of fulfillment and humane navigation.

### Addition to Chapter Four: Behavioral Markers of the Five Lenses

I recommend adding this section to Chapter Four after the description of the five lenses of perception but before the "Role of GCT in Restoring Balance" section (around page 52-53).

## Behavioral Markers of the Five Lenses

While the theoretical description of the five lenses provides a conceptual framework, clinicians need concrete, observable markers to identify which lens is currently active in a client's presentation. The following behavioral indicators offer practical guidance for recognizing the specific manifestations of each lens in clinical settings.

### The Critic Lens: Observable Markers

#### Verbal Indicators:

- Uses absolute terms like "always," "never," "should," and "must"
- Employs harsh self-descriptors ("I'm worthless," "I'm a failure")
- Compares self unfavorably to others ("Everyone else can handle this")
- Dismisses accomplishments and amplifies shortcomings
- Speaks in a judgmental tone about self and sometimes others

#### Nonverbal Indicators:

- Slumped posture with shoulders drawn inward
- Downward gaze or avoidance of eye contact
- Facial micro-expressions of contempt (usually self-directed)
- Tension in the jaw and around the eyes
- Nervous self-touching or self-soothing behaviors

- Voice becomes higher-pitched or strained

**Physiological Markers:**

- Shallow breathing centered in upper chest
- Increased heart rate during self-critical thoughts
- Tension headaches and neck stiffness
- Gastrointestinal distress related to self-judgment

**Behavioral Patterns:**

- Excessive checking and rechecking work
- Apologizing unnecessarily or excessively
- Seeking reassurance while simultaneously rejecting it
- Avoiding situations where "failure" might occur
- Procrastination driven by fear of imperfection
- Overworking to compensate for perceived inadequacy

**Clinical Example:** During therapy, Melissa reviews her week and immediately focuses on a minor error in a work presentation. Her shoulders hunch, voice tightens, and she uses phrases like "I always mess up the important details" despite evidence to the contrary. When the therapist points out the presentation's success, she quickly dismisses this, saying "I should have done better." These markers clearly indicate the critic lens is active.

## The Bully Lens: Observable Markers

### Verbal Indicators:

- Uses accusatory language ("You made me feel this way")
- Employs aggressive or defensive speech patterns
- Externalizes blame for difficulties
- Justifies problematic behavior ("I had no choice but to react that way")
- Uses dismissive language about others' perspectives

### Nonverbal Indicators:

- Rigid, expansive posture or territorial body positioning
- Intense or confrontational eye contact
- Facial expressions of anger or contempt
- Pointing gestures or other dominating hand movements
- Increased volume and forceful speech patterns
- Forward-leaning body orientation

### Physiological Markers:

- Flushed face or neck
- Visible tension in arms and hands
- Shallow, rapid breathing
- Increased animation and movement during confrontational topics

**Behavioral Patterns:**

- Interrupts others or dominates conversations
- Difficulty receiving feedback without counterattacking
- Pattern of strained or broken relationships
- Controlling behaviors in interpersonal dynamics
- Quick escalation from minor frustrations to significant anger
- Difficulty acknowledging impact of behavior on others

**Clinical Example:** When discussing a conflict with his partner, James's posture becomes rigid, voice loudens, and he leans forward aggressively. His face flushes as he states, "She always tries to control me. If she'd just back off, we wouldn't have these problems." He interrupts the therapist's gentle exploration and justifies his angry outburst as "the only way to get her to listen." These markers clearly indicate the bully lens is active.

**The Mediator Lens: Observable Markers**

**Verbal Indicators:**

- Uses placating language ("Whatever you think is best")
- Frequently agrees without genuine conviction
- Qualifies statements to avoid taking clear positions
- Focuses on others' needs while minimizing personal ones
- Overuses phrases like "I'm fine" or "It doesn't matter"

**Nonverbal Indicators:**

- Appeasing smile that doesn't reach the eyes
- Nodding excessively while others speak
- Open-handed gestures that suggest surrender
- Body positioned to appear smaller or non-threatening
- Facial expressions that mask true emotions
- Voice modulation to sound agreeable

**Physiological Markers:**

- Controlled, shallow breathing
- Muscular tension with outward appearance of relaxation
- Stress responses activated while appearing calm
- Fatigue from constant emotional regulation

**Behavioral Patterns:**

- Difficulty articulating personal wants or needs
- Abandons personal boundaries when challenged
- Chronic indecisiveness about personal preferences
- Pattern of resentment following self-sacrifice
- Emotional exhaustion from peace-keeping efforts
- Indirect expression of needs through hints or passive behaviors

**Clinical Example:** During couples therapy, Lisa consistently defers to her partner's preferences. When asked about her own desires, she smiles tightly and says, "I'm happy with whatever makes him happy." Her body appears relaxed, but the therapist notices her hands clenched under the table. When her partner leaves to use the restroom, her shoulders immediately drop and she sighs deeply. These markers clearly indicate the mediator lens is active.

**The Counselor Lens: Observable Markers**

**Verbal Indicators:**

- Uses analytical or intellectualized language
- Speaks about emotions rather than expressing them
- Employs psychological terminology to distance from experience
- Presents logical analyses of emotional situations
- Uses third-person perspective when discussing personal issues

**Nonverbal Indicators:**

- Maintains composed facial expressions during emotional content
- Limited emotional expressivity or flat affect
- Gestures that emphasize logical points rather than emotional ones
- Physical stillness or controlled movements
- Facial animation primarily during intellectual discussions

**Physiological Markers:**

- Controlled breathing patterns
- Limited physiological responsiveness during emotional topics
- Physical disconnection from emotional content
- Tension in forehead (thinking) rather than chest/abdomen (feeling)

**Behavioral Patterns:**

- Researches problems extensively rather than addressing emotions
- Offers advice to others while struggling to apply it personally
- Creates elaborate plans that lack emotional engagement
- Difficulty with spontaneity or emotional improvisation
- Seeks understanding without accompanying emotional processing
- Uses helping others as avoidance of personal issues

**Clinical Example:** When exploring his grief over his father's death, Marcus speaks articulately about the "five stages of grief" and analyzes which stage he believes he's experiencing. His breathing remains measured, facial expression composed. When the therapist gently notes that he hasn't mentioned how he feels, Marcus replies, "I understand that expressing emotion is important for processing grief." His body remains still, with tension visible primarily in his forehead. These markers clearly indicate the counselor lens is active.

**The Heart Lens: Observable Markers**

**Verbal Indicators:**

- Uses authentic "I" statements that own experience
- Expresses emotions directly but non-reactively
- Acknowledges multiple perspectives without losing personal truth
- Speaks with nuance rather than absolutism
- Balances emotional honesty with thoughtful reflection

**Nonverbal Indicators:**

- Open, balanced posture that is neither collapsed nor rigid
- Natural, connected eye contact
- Facial expressions that match verbal content
- Fluid, organic gestures that emphasize meaning
- Voice modulation that reflects authentic feeling without overwhelm
- Hand movements that often reference the chest/heart area

**Physiological Markers:**

- Deep, diaphragmatic breathing
- Coherent heart rate variability patterns
- Relaxed yet engaged physical presence
- Emotional arousal without dysregulation

- Capacity to maintain bodily awareness during emotional content

**Behavioral Patterns:**

- Responds rather than reacts to challenging situations
- Sets boundaries with compassion rather than aggression
- Acknowledges mistakes without excessive self-criticism
- Remains present during difficult emotions
- Makes decisions that honor both self and others
- Demonstrates flexibility without abandoning core values

**Clinical Example:** When discussing a difficult conversation with her daughter, Susan speaks with emotional honesty: "I felt hurt when she criticized my parenting, and I'm trying to understand her perspective while also honoring my own experience." Her breathing remains deep and even, body posture open yet grounded. She touches her heart area when expressing deeper emotions but maintains composure. When the therapist asks a challenging question, she pauses thoughtfully before responding. These markers clearly indicate the heart lens is active.

**Clinical Application: Tracking Lens Transitions**

Therapists should pay particular attention to the transitions between lenses, as these shifts often reveal important clinical information:

**Critic to Bully Transition:**

- Often triggered when self-criticism is too painful to maintain

- Marked by sudden externalization of blame
- Physical shift from collapsed to rigid posture
- Therapeutic opportunity to explore vulnerability beneath defenses

**Mediator to Critic Transition:**

- Typically occurs when peace-keeping fails
- Self-blame emerges for inability to maintain harmony
- Physical manifestation of collapsed posture and inward focus
- Therapeutic opportunity to strengthen authentic self-expression

**Counselor to Heart Transition:**

- Characterized by shift from intellectual to emotional language
- Often accompanied by deeper breathing and increased color in face
- Voice may become more resonant or emotionally expressive
- Therapeutic goal to reinforce this transition without overwhelming client

**Documentation Tips for Lens Identification:**

When documenting lens activity in session notes, consider using a simple coding system:

- CL: Critic Lens active

- BL: Bully Lens active
- ML: Mediator Lens active
- COL: Counselor Lens active
- HL: Heart Lens active

Example progress note: "Client initially presented with CL when discussing work performance (self-critical language, hunched posture). When exploring childhood influences, shifted to COL (intellectualized emotional content, limited affect). Brief HL activation when discussing creative pursuits (authentic expression, open posture, deeper breathing)."

Tracking these patterns over time provides valuable data about the client's progress toward heart-centered alignment.

**Intervention Strategies Based on Identified Lens**

**When Critic Lens is Dominant:**

- Activate the observer to create distance from self-criticism
- Guide client to place hand on heart while repeating self-compassionate statement
- Use empty chair technique to dialogue with critic part
- Assign "evidence gathering" homework that counters global negative self-judgments

**When Bully Lens is Dominant:**

- Use grounding techniques to reduce physiological arousal
- Explore vulnerability beneath defensive anger
- Practice perspective-taking exercises to develop empathy

- Teach response delay strategies to interrupt reactive patterns

**When Mediator Lens is Dominant:**

- Practice direct expression of preferences starting with low-risk scenarios
- Explore fear of conflict that drives appeasing behaviors
- Teach distinction between healthy compromise and self-abandonment
- Use body-awareness exercises to identify suppressed emotions

**When Counselor Lens is Dominant:**

- Bridge intellectual insights with emotional experience
- Use somatic techniques to increase body awareness
- Practice "feeling the feeling" before analyzing it
- Assign expressive arts activities that bypass analytical processing

**When Heart Lens Emerges:**

- Reinforce this state through explicit acknowledgment
- Help client anchor the experience somatically for future recall
- Explore what facilitated this shift to replicate in daily life
- Create practice opportunities to strengthen this lens outside sessions

By recognizing these specific behavioral markers, therapists can precisely identify which lens is currently active and tailor interventions accordingly. This observation-based approach enhances therapeutic effectiveness by addressing the exact pattern of misalignment present in the moment, rather than applying general techniques that may not match the client's current state.

## Supplementary Discussion: Integrating Theory and Practice

To further enrich the understanding of GCT, it is helpful to integrate additional theoretical perspectives and practical considerations that extend beyond the immediate framework. This supplementary section offers expanded commentary on how the core concepts of GCT relate to broader trends in trauma psychology, neuroscience, and embodied therapies.

## Integrating Neuroscience and Embodied Healing

Recent advances in neuroscience have underscored the importance of the mind–body connection in healing trauma. Research on heart coherence (McCraty et al., 2015) and the Polyvagal Theory (Porges, 2011) supports the notion that our physiological state is intimately connected to our emotional and psychological well-being. In GCT, the recognition of the heart's powerful electromagnetic field is not merely metaphorical—it reflects a measurable phenomenon that influences emotional regulation and cognitive function. By fostering practices that promote heart coherence, such as deep breathing, meditation, and biofeedback, therapists can help clients shift from states dominated by ego reactivity to those characterized by balanced, heart-led awareness.

## The Role of Narrative in Healing

Another key component of GCT is the therapeutic use of narrative. Clients are encouraged to reframe their personal stories, shifting from narratives of failure and isolation to ones that emphasize resilience and connection. This narrative reframing is supported by research in trauma psychology that highlights the importance of meaning-making in the healing process (Neimeyer, 2001). By re-authoring their life stories, clients can dismantle the pervasive influence of ego solarism and embrace a narrative that honors their authentic self.

### Embracing the Complexity of the Psyche

The human psyche is complex and multifaceted. GCT acknowledges this complexity by not reducing the psyche to a single element but by embracing the dynamic interplay between the observer, spirit, ego, and heart. This holistic perspective is vital, as it aligns with contemporary understandings of psychological resilience that emphasize the integration of multiple layers of experience (Bonanno, 2004). By recognizing and validating the full spectrum of human experience, GCT provides a framework that is both compassionate and clinically robust.

### Practical Implications for Clinicians

For clinicians, the practical application of GCT requires both sensitivity and skill. It involves:

**Active Listening:**
Attuning to the client's narrative with an open, nonjudgmental stance.

**Facilitating Mindfulness:**
Introducing practices that help clients cultivate the Observer's neutrality.

**Encouraging Embodiment:**
Incorporating somatic techniques that support the integration of body and mind.

**Supporting Narrative Reframing:**
Guiding clients to articulate and reframe their personal stories, thereby unlocking new pathways for healing.

By integrating these approaches, clinicians can create a therapeutic environment that not only addresses symptoms but also fosters long-term growth and intentional evolution.

**Final Conclusion**

This chapter has provided a comprehensive exploration of the foundational concepts of Gifted Compassionate Therapy. Through detailed discussion of the core components—the observer, spirit, ego, and heart—and the dynamic interplay between them, we have outlined how GCT addresses the distortions of ego solarism and the weight of spiritual gravity. By using the alignment equations ($E + Hc = \downarrow S$ and $E^2 - Hc = \uparrow S$) as guiding principles, GCT reveals how suffering can be reduced and genuine healing achieved.

Furthermore, by exploring the five lenses of perception and addressing life's five existential questions, GCT offers a practical roadmap for individuals seeking to reclaim their authentic selves. Whether through clinical practice or personal exploration, the principles outlined in this chapter empower individuals to move beyond reactive patterns, embrace intentional evolution, and ultimately live with clarity, connection, and compassion.

**Integration and Synthesis of GCT**

As you continue your journey with Gifted Compassionate Therapy, remember that the path to healing is not linear. It is a dynamic process that invites continual self-reflection, integration, and growth—a process in which every experience, every challenge, and every insight contributes to a richer, more aligned existence.

The foundational concepts we have explored—ego-solarism, the alignment equation, the five lenses of perception, and life's five big questions—provide the theoretical architecture of Gifted Compassionate Therapy. Together, they create a comprehensive map of the human psyche and its pathways to intentional evolution. However, theory alone is insufficient for clinical practice. To effectively guide clients toward alignment, therapists need practical methods to assess where clients currently stand on their journey.

In Chapter Five, we translate these foundational concepts into clinical assessment tools. The intake process and diagnostic framework of GCT are designed not to label or pathologize clients, but to illuminate their unique patterns of misalignment and potential for growth. These assessment methods reveal how ego-solarism manifests in individual clients, which egoic lenses dominate their perception, and what specific interventions might facilitate their realignment with the heart's wisdom.

As we explore these diagnostic approaches, consider how they differ from traditional assessment models. Rather than reducing clients to diagnostic categories, GCT's assessment framework honors the whole person while providing clear direction for therapeutic intervention. This approach transforms diagnosis from a static label into a dynamic roadmap for intentional evolution.

# Chapter Five
# Intake Assessment and Diagnostic Tools

## Introduction

In Gifted Compassionate Therapy (GCT), diagnostic tools serve a transformative purpose: to uncover an individual's authentic internal state by bypassing the ego's narrative and exposing deeper emotional patterns and self-care tendencies. Unlike traditional psychological assessments that rely primarily on self-reported data, GCT employs projective diagnostics and functional analyses to reveal discrepancies between how individuals perceive themselves and their true state of alignment on the journey toward healing (Vecchio, 2025). This innovative approach utilizes historical models of self-assessment and integrates recent advances in trauma research and neuropsychology to create a more holistic picture of the psyche.

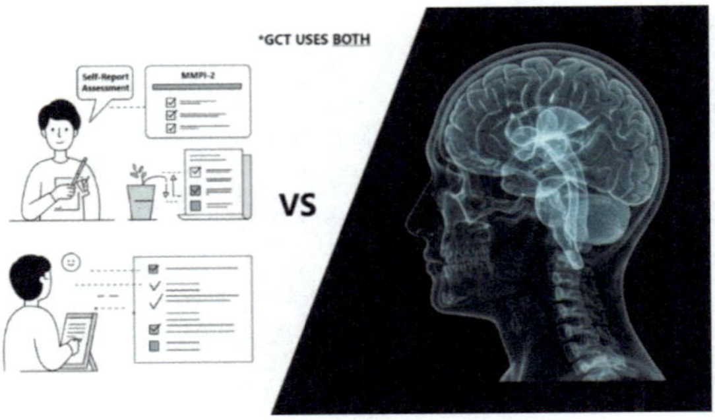

Conventional assessments such as the Minnesota Multiphasic Personality Inventory (MMPI-2) are designed to produce personality profiles based on self-reports, yet these profiles are often influenced by the ego's desire to present a socially favorable image (Wright & Simms, 2015). Moreover, traditional tools typically disregard subclinical patterns—traits that fall below diagnostic thresholds but reveal significant adaptive or maladaptive strategies. In contrast, GCT recognizes these patterns as critical indicators of internal misalignment and potential growth. By emphasizing alignment rather than pathology, GCT offers a revolutionary approach that highlights intentional evolution and the restoration of balance.

*Transitional Note:*
As you read, consider not only how these diagnostic tools map the individual's current state but also how they serve as a guide for intentional evolution. The framework laid out in this chapter bridges theoretical foundations (as established in Chapters 1–3) with later, more detailed therapeutic interventions.

## 4.1 Purpose of Diagnostics in GCT

The primary purpose of GCT's diagnostic tools is to map an individual's alignment with the 10 Absolute Truths and the Humane Spectrum—two core frames of reference that guide intentional evolution (Vecchio, 2025). Rather than simply labeling symptoms or categorizing behaviors (as is common in conventional assessments, American Psychiatric Association, 2013), GCT diagnostics emphasize how individuals navigate both their internal and external worlds. This approach reveals where a person lies on the humane spectrum, highlighting areas of disconnection and pinpointing opportunities for growth.

## The Unique Role of Internal Self-Care

One of GCT's groundbreaking contributions is its focus on measuring internal self-care. Traditional models rely on self-reported measures, which can be skewed by the ego's need to present an ideal image. In contrast, GCT employs projective diagnostics to access the unconscious patterns underlying self-care practices. For example, while many professionals may claim that they practice compromise as a form of self-care (with research suggesting approximately 24% adopt compromise as their primary conflict strategy; American Psychiatric Association, 2013), GCT diagnostics might reveal that such compromise masks deeper tendencies of self-neglect under stress.

*Case Insight:*
Imagine a client who asserts that they care for themselves by always prioritizing collaboration. Under stress, however, GCT assessment reveals that this individual tends to submit and suppress personal needs in order to avoid conflict. Recognizing this hidden pattern allows for a reframing of self-care, enabling a shift from unconscious compromise to conscious, compassionate self-support.

**Reflective Prompt:**
Reflect on a client who may have presented an overly positive self-image in traditional assessments. How might projective diagnostics uncover hidden patterns of self-neglect or misalignment?

**Summary:**
GCT diagnostics are designed to uncover not just the overt symptoms but also the subtle, subclinical patterns that drive an individual's internal state—providing a comprehensive map for intentional evolution.

## 4.2 GCT's Diagnostic Framework

GCT's diagnostic framework is built on the philosophy of intentional evolution and is designed to reveal the deeper mechanisms driving behavior. It integrates three core elements: projective measures, functional analysis, and alignment mapping. Together, these elements provide a multidimensional understanding of the psyche that goes well beyond conventional assessments (Vecchio, 2025; Wright & Simms, 2015).

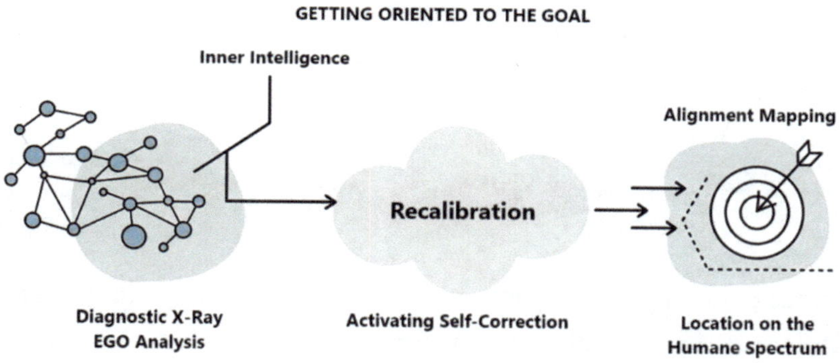


### 1. Projective Measures

Projective diagnostics are central to the GCT approach because they bypass the ego's distortions by eliciting unconscious responses. Tools such as ambiguous image interpretation or narrative exercises reveal hidden patterns of thought, emotion, and behavior that are inaccessible through direct self-reporting. This method is akin to, yet distinct from, classical projective assessments like the Rorschach or Thematic Apperception Test, as it specifically focuses on aspects of self-care and alignment.

**2. Functional Analysis**

Functional analysis in GCT evaluates how individuals adapt to life's challenges, emphasizing self-care preferences and instinctual responses. Instead of simply labeling behaviors as pathological, this analysis examines their adaptive function—revealing whether a given strategy (such as compromise) is truly beneficial or is masking deeper disconnection. This nuanced analysis often incorporates elements of both qualitative interviews and standardized observation.

**3. Alignment Mapping**

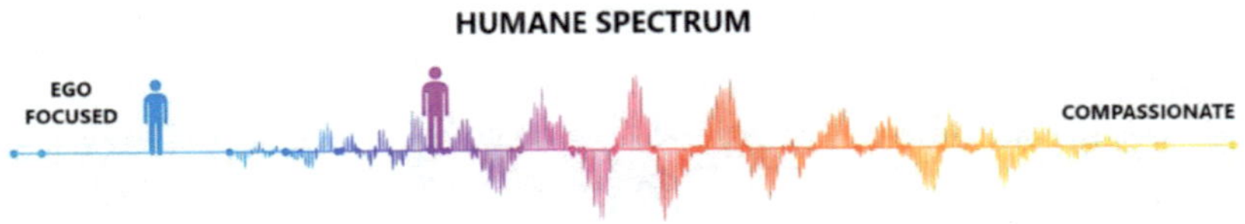


Alignment mapping instruments are used to identify an individual's placement on a Humane Spectrum. This mapping process is dynamic and allows for tracking changes over time. It not only diagnoses current misalignments but also informs treatment planning by highlighting specific areas for intentional intervention. The map serves as a roadmap for both the client and therapist, guiding the journey toward intentional evolution. Importantly, this mapping carries absolutely no diagnostic stigma

*Expanded Theoretical Integration:*
Traditional diagnostic models often dismiss subclinical traits as irrelevant; however, GCT argues that even subtle deviations from alignment can have significant cumulative effects. By incorporating insights from systems theory and indigenous models of holistic health, GCT's framework acknowledges that

every aspect of behavior—no matter how minor—can impact overall balance.

**Reflective Prompt:**
Consider how a multidimensional framework that includes projective measures and functional analysis might reveal insights missed by standard assessments. How can these insights be used to tailor interventions more precisely?

**Summary:**
The GCT diagnostic framework, with its emphasis on projective measures, functional analysis, and alignment mapping, offers a transformative, integrative view of the psyche that prioritizes growth and intentional evolution over mere symptom categorization.

### 4.3 Uniqueness of GCT's Approach

GCT's diagnostic approach is distinctive in its ability to bypass ego distortions, focus on growth potential, and integrate seamlessly with therapeutic goals. This section highlights three innovative aspects that set GCT apart from traditional models.

### Bypassing Ego Distortions

Traditional assessments (e.g., MMPI-2) rely on self-reporting, which can be heavily influenced by the ego's desire to conform to social expectations (Wright & Simms, 2015). GCT's projective methods, however, access unconscious patterns that reveal the client's true internal state. This bypass of ego distortions allows therapists to see beyond the facade and understand the underlying adaptive or maladaptive strategies.

**Transforming Compromise into Compassion**

Many individuals unconsciously practice compromise, often suppressing their own needs to maintain harmony. Although such compromise may be seen as positive, it often indicates a deeper misalignment—one that perpetuates suffering. GCT's diagnostic tools help transform this unconscious compromise into active, conscious compassion. By revealing the discrepancy between reported behaviors and authentic self-care practices, GCT guides clients toward strategies that foster genuine self-compassion and alignment (Vecchio, 2025).

**Identifying and Nurturing Gifted Compassionates**

One of the most innovative contributions of GCT is its ability to identify true "gifted compassionates"—individuals who possess a heightened capacity for empathy and compassion but may also be vulnerable to emotional overwhelm. GCT helps these individuals reframe their sensitivity as a strength, nurturing their potential to lead with compassion. This not only supports individual healing but also contributes to building more humane, connected communities (McCraty et al., 2015).

**Reflective Prompt:**
Think about a client who, on the surface, appears highly agreeable but may be sacrificing their own needs. How could GCT's approach reveal the underlying dynamics and support the client in transforming compromise into conscious compassion?

**Summary:**
GCT's innovative diagnostic approach—through its bypassing of ego distortions, transformation of compromise, and identification of gifted compassionates—provides a rich, multidimensional perspective that sets the stage for intentional evolution.

## 4.4 Collaborative Nature of Diagnostics in GCT

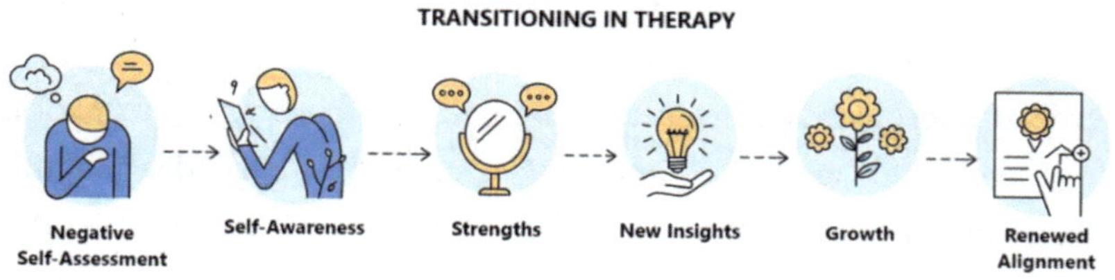


A central tenet of GCT is that diagnostics should be a collaborative process—one that engages the client in uncovering their true internal state. Traditional diagnostic tools measure how individuals *report* themselves and label them accordingly, whereas GCT's approach reveals their authentic state by examining unconscious patterns and stress responses.

### Ego Distortions and Stress as Revealing Factors

Under conditions of stress or conflict, the ego's defenses can weaken, causing previously subclinical patterns to emerge. For example, in standard MMPI-2 profiles, certain peaks may remain below clinical thresholds during baseline functioning but become pronounced under stress. GCT's projective diagnostics capture these dynamic shifts, providing critical insights into the client's true adaptive strategies.

*Case Insight:*
Consider a client who consistently describes themselves as collaborative and empathetic. Yet, when faced with conflict, their behavior shifts dramatically toward avoidance or defensiveness. GCT's collaborative process identifies this discrepancy, allowing the therapist to work with the client on addressing the underlying fears and realigning their behavior with their authentic self-care values.

### A Dialogical Process

GCT diagnostics are inherently collaborative. Rather than being a one-sided assessment, the process involves a dialogue between therapist and client. Therapists share insights from projective tools and functional analyses, and together they map the client's placement on the Humane Spectrum. This co-creative process not only demystifies the diagnostic process but also empowers clients to take ownership of their journey toward intentional evolution rather than reduce them to a label.

### Practical Implications for Therapy

The collaborative nature of GCT's diagnostics yields several practical benefits:

- **Identifying Misalignment:** Revealing unconscious patterns that might otherwise remain hidden.
- **Empowering Clients:** Helping clients reframe their internal experiences and recognize their capacity for self-care.
- **Informing Treatment:** Integrating diagnostic insights into personalized treatment planning that targets areas for growth.

**Reflective Prompt:**
How might involving clients more directly in the diagnostic process enhance their commitment to change? Consider ways to structure feedback sessions that invite collaborative exploration of diagnostic insights.

**Summary:**
GCT's collaborative diagnostic process fosters a shared understanding between therapist and client, enhancing the overall

therapeutic alliance and supporting meaningful, intentional evolution.

### 4.5 Sample Assessment Tools and Protocols

To translate GCT's diagnostic framework into clinical practice, therapists need concrete tools that capture the nuanced interplay between the observer, spirit, ego, and heart. The following assessment instruments can be adapted for your practice to create a comprehensive picture of client misalignment and potential for growth.

## The GCT Intake Assessment Protocol

Below is a structured intake protocol that integrates both projective and functional measures:

**Section 1: Cognitive Style Assessment**

- Hemisphere Dominance: □ Left-brain dominant □ Right-brain dominant □ Balanced
- Learning Style: □ Visual □ Auditory □ Kinesthetic □ Mixed
- Processing Preference: □ Sequential/Analytical □ Global/Intuitive
- Previous Neuropsychological Test Scores (if available):
    - Verbal Comprehension Index: _____
    - Perceptual Reasoning Index: _____
    - Working Memory Index: _____
    - Processing Speed Index: _____

**Section 2: Self-Care Preference Inventory** Rate each response on a scale of 1 (never) to 5 (always)

When facing conflict or challenge, I tend to:

1. Fight back directly (Confrontation) _____
2. Avoid the situation entirely (Avoidance) _____
3. Give in to maintain peace (Submission) _____
4. Find middle ground even at personal cost (Compromise) _____
5. Seek solutions that meet everyone's needs (Collaboration) _____

**Section 3: Affective Pairings Assessment** Check the emotional pairings that most frequently occur together: □ Anger—Shame □ Sadness—Guilt □ Fear—Helplessness □ Joy—Anxiety (inability to sustain positive emotions) □ Other significant pairings: ___________________

**Section 4: Egoic Lens Dominance Survey** Rate each statement on a scale of 1 (strongly disagree) to 5 (strongly agree)

Critic Lens:

- I often find fault with myself even for small mistakes _____
- I hold myself to standards that I wouldn't expect of others _____
- I frequently replay my errors in my mind _____

Bully Lens:

- When threatened, I tend to become defensive or aggressive _____
- I often blame others for problems or difficulties _____
- I have a strong need to control situations or people _____

Mediator Lens:

- I frequently sacrifice my needs to keep peace _____
- I avoid expressing my true feelings to prevent conflict _____
- I find it difficult to take a firm stance on issues _____

Counselor Lens:

- I overanalyze situations before taking action _____
- I intellectualize emotions rather than feeling them _____
- I prefer rational solutions over emotional processing _____

Heart Lens:

- I can remain compassionate even during conflict _____
- I trust my intuitive insights about situations _____
- I can distinguish between immediate emotions and deeper values _____

**Section 5: Humane Spectrum Placement**

Based on the assessment, the client appears to be located at: □ Predominantly Egocentric (Critic/Bully dominant) □ Moderately Egocentric (Critic/Mediator dominant) □ Transitional (Mixed dominance with emerging heart awareness) □ Moderately Heart-Centered (Heart lens emerging with ego integration) □ Predominantly Heart-Centered (Heart as primary compass)

## Projective Assessment: The Life Mapping Exercise

This projective technique helps bypass ego defenses to reveal unconscious patterns. Provide clients with paper and drawing materials, then guide them through this exercise:

**Instructions for Therapists:**

1. Ask the client to draw a visual map of their life journey, including:
    - A starting point (birth)
    - A current location (present moment)
    - Significant milestones or turning points
    - Obstacles or challenges
    - Resources or supports
    - Future directions or goals
2. Observe not only the content but also:
    - Where the client places emphasis (size, color, detail)
    - What areas they avoid or minimize
    - The overall organization (linear, circular, fragmented)
    - Symbols or metaphors that emerge
3. After completion, ask exploratory questions:
    - "What gives you strength on this journey?"
    - "Where do you feel most connected to your heart on this map?"
    - "Which challenges have shaped who you are today?"
    - "If your heart could add something to this map, what would it be?"

**Interpretation Guide:**

| **Element** | **Potential Significance** | **Connection to GCT** |
|---|---|---|
| Map organization | Linear/structured = left-brain dominance; Circular/flowing = right-brain dominance | Indicates cognitive style and potential interventions |
| Size of elements | Larger items often represent emotional significance or egoic fixation | Reveals which experiences have shaped egoic lenses |
| Empty spaces | May represent avoidance, unconscious material, or disconnection | Areas where the observer has not integrated experience |
| Bridges/pathways | Represent transitions or connections between experiences | Potential areas for heart-centered integration |
| Colors used | Emotional tone and affective states | Insight into spirit's expression and emotional patterns |
| Future orientation | Degree of hope, direction, clarity about purpose | Indicates heart connection and intentional evolution capacity |

## The Heart-Ego Alignment Scale (HEAS)

This self-report measure helps quantify the client's current state of alignment. It can be administered at intake and periodically throughout treatment to track progress.

**Instructions:** Rate each statement on a scale from 1 (never true) to 5 (always true)

1. I can observe my thoughts without becoming completely identified with them
2. I recognize when my inner critic is speaking versus my authentic self
3. When making decisions, I consult my heart (intuition) as well as my mind
4. I can feel difficult emotions without becoming overwhelmed by them
5. I notice when I'm operating from fear versus from love or compassion
6. I catch myself when I'm blaming others for my experiences
7. I can maintain my center during interpersonal conflicts
8. I recognize the difference between reactive emotions and present-moment feelings
9. I can distinguish between my ego's desires and my heart's wisdom
10. I forgive myself when I make mistakes
11. I can sit with uncertainty without needing immediate resolution
12. I recognize when I'm seeking external validation versus internal alignment

13. I can witness my suffering without identifying completely with it
14. I'm aware of how my past experiences shape my current perceptions
15. I can experience joy without immediately fearing its loss

**Scoring:**

- 15-30: Predominantly Ego-Driven (Strong ego solarism)
- 31-45: Ego-Oriented with Moments of Heart Connection
- 46-60: Transitional (Growing heart alignment with ego integration)
- 61-75: Predominantly Heart-Centered

## Instinctual Impairment Assessment

This structured interview helps identify areas where natural instincts have been compromised by trauma, conditioning, or egoic distortions.

**Interview Questions:**

Trust Instinct:

1. "How easily do you form trust with new people in your life?"
2. "What signals help you determine whether someone is trustworthy?"
3. "Have there been times when you trusted someone despite internal warning signs?"

Safety Instinct:

1. "How do you recognize when you're in an emotionally unsafe situation?"
2. "What physical sensations arise when you feel threatened?"
3. "Do you find yourself in repeatedly unsafe relationships or situations?"

Intimacy Instinct:

1. "How comfortable are you with emotional closeness to others?"
2. "What happens in your body when someone tries to get emotionally close to you?"
3. "Do you find yourself creating distance in relationships when they deepen?"

Self-Preservation Instinct:

1. "How effectively do you recognize and meet your own needs?"
2. "What happens when you need to set boundaries with others?"
3. "Do you prioritize others' needs at the expense of your wellbeing?"

**Scoring Guide:**

For each instinct, rate impairment on a scale of 1-5:

1. Minimal impairment (instinct functions optimally)
2. Mild impairment (occasional difficulty)

3. Moderate impairment (frequent difficulty)
4. Severe impairment (instinct significantly compromised)
5. Profound impairment (instinct barely functional)

This assessment provides critical insight into which instinctual areas require healing and realignment.

## Implementation in Practice

These assessment tools are designed to be used flexibly within your clinical practice. They may be administered across multiple sessions, with sections prioritized based on client presentation and therapeutic focus. The integration of data from these various tools provides a comprehensive map of the client's internal landscape—identifying not only areas of suffering but also pathways for alignment and growth.

The assessment process itself is therapeutic, as it activates the observer and begins to familiarize clients with the language of heart-centered awareness. As clients engage with these tools, they often experience initial insights into their patterns of misalignment and glimpse the possibility of intentional evolution.

### Integration and Synthesis

To synthesize the diverse elements of GCT's diagnostic approach, consider how each component contributes to a unified framework of intentional evolution. Diagnostics in GCT do more than measure; they reveal the internal dynamics that underlie behavior, expose the gaps between perceived and authentic self-care strategies, and offer a roadmap for transformation.

Intentional evolution teaches us that every moment of misalignment—every instance where the ego distorts the true self—contains the potential for growth. By collaboratively engaging with diagnostic data, therapists can help clients:

- Recognize the subtle patterns of misalignment.
- Transform unconscious compromise into conscious compassion.
- Harness the power of their internal adaptive mechanisms for intentional growth.

This integrative process not only informs individualized treatment but also points toward broader implications for community and organizational health. As diagnostic insights accumulate, they can guide systemic interventions that promote a more humane and connected society.

**Reflective Prompt:**
How do the various elements of GCT's diagnostic process come together to support a client's journey toward alignment? In what ways might these insights inform broader systemic change in your field?

**Future Directions:**
Emerging research in neuroplasticity, heart coherence, and trauma-informed care promises to further refine these diagnostic approaches. As GCT evolves, integrating new findings will deepen our understanding and enhance the effectiveness of these transformative tools.

### Conclusion and Transitional Note

Diagnostic tools in Gifted Compassionate Therapy are not merely instruments of measurement; they are vehicles for transformation.

By bypassing the ego's distortions and uncovering authentic internal patterns, GCT diagnostics provide a comprehensive roadmap for alignment, intentional evolution, and meaningful growth. This chapter has detailed the unique framework of GCT diagnostics—from the purpose and theoretical underpinnings to the collaborative processes and practical implications. The insights gained here set the stage for subsequent chapters, where these diagnostic insights will inform concrete therapeutic interventions and treatment planning.

*Transitional Note:*
As you move forward, consider how the diagnostic insights discussed here can be integrated into your clinical practice. In the next chapter, we will explore practical frameworks and interventions that build upon these diagnostic foundations, guiding both individual and systemic transformation.

# Chapter Six
# Practical Framework for GCT

## Introduction

Gifted Compassionate Therapy (GCT) is grounded in universal truths that reveal the human condition and the path to alignment. These truths elucidate how separation, division, and suffering shape the psyche while simultaneously offering a roadmap to intentional evolution. Central to GCT's framework are the **10 Absolute Truths**—a developmental sequence that captures the shared human experience and establishes a philosophical foundation for understanding the psyche's natural self-corrective design. In embracing these truths, individuals begin to view suffering not as a flaw but as a signal for growth and transformation.

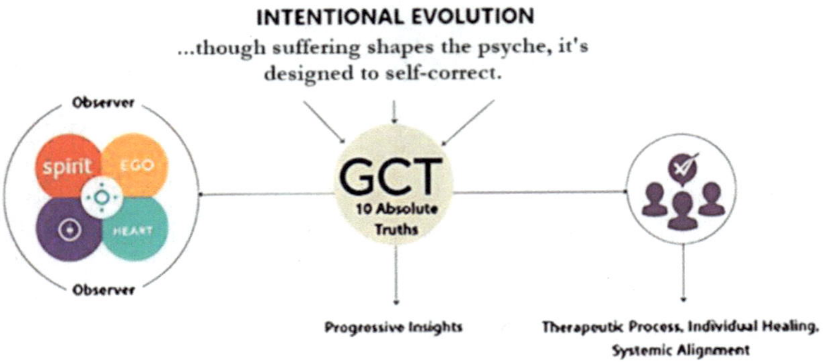

This chapter will:

- Outline the 10 Absolute Truths that form the philosophical foundation of GCT.
- Explore the progressive insights that naturally arise from alignment.
- Demonstrate how these truths and insights underpin the therapeutic process, guiding both individual healing and systemic change.

Throughout this chapter, historical context, extended clinical vignettes, reflective prompts, and practical session outlines are integrated so that therapists may readily apply these principles in their work. As you read, consider how the framework presented here might inform you of your approach to fostering intentional evolution in clients and, ultimately, contribute to broader systemic transformation.

*Transitional Note:*
The ideas outlined here build upon the foundational work in Chapters 1–4 and set the stage for the detailed diagnostic and intervention strategies described in later chapters.

## 5.1 The 10 Absolute Truths: A Map for Intentional Evolution

The **10 Absolute Truths** articulate the universal developmental sequence of the human psyche. They explain how adaptive angst arises from division and how re-centering with the heart resolves suffering. In the following sections, each truth is discussed in depth with theoretical elaboration, practical examples, and reflective prompts.

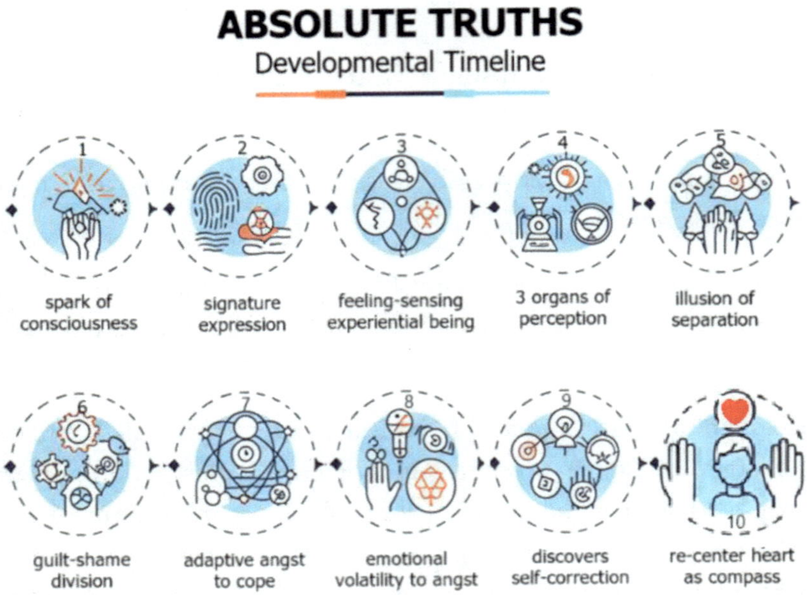


1. **Everyone begins as a spark of consciousness, a hopeful expectation for the future.**
   At the very start, every human is imbued with a vibrant spark—a concentrated expression of pure potential. This spark symbolizes the inherent capacity for growth, connection, and creative contribution. Historically, ancient traditions celebrated the "inner light" as the essence of life; modern neuroscience similarly reveals that early neural connectivity lays the groundwork for later cognitive and emotional development.
   *Reflective Prompt:* Consider a time when you recognized a child's unfiltered curiosity. How might that spark of consciousness serve as a model for intentional evolution in adulthood?

2.

3. **Everyone carries a concentrated signature expression of consciousness, uniquely their own.**
   Each individual's essence is singular and unique. This signature not only distinguishes us from one another but also serves as the basis for personal purpose and direction. The uniqueness of our consciousness is what drives creativity and personal expression.
   *Reflective Prompt:* Reflect on a client's distinctive way of relating to the world. How can recognizing their uniqueness foster self-acceptance and intentional growth?

4. **Everyone is a feeling-sensing-experiential being, reacting to the present moment.**
   Before language and ego take shape, human beings experience life in its raw form through sensations and feelings. This immediate, pre-reflective mode of engagement allows for a deep connection with the present. Over time, however, external influences and internal narratives may obscure these pure experiences.
   *Reflective Prompt:* In your clinical work, how might you help clients rediscover the immediacy of their sensory and emotional experiences?

5. **Everyone has three organs of perception: spirit (feelings), ego (adaptive function), and heart (human compass).**
   These three components—spirit, ego, and heart—constitute the core framework of human perception. The spirit captures our immediate, raw emotional experiences; the ego organizes and adapts these experiences to external demands; and the heart serves as the authentic guide, integrating both emotional and intuitive wisdom.
   *Reflective Prompt:* How can you assist clients in recognizing

the distinct roles of their spirit, ego, and heart during moments of distress?

6. **Everyone undergoes the illusion of separation from their intelligent spark of consciousness.**
   Early life experiences—such as rejection, trauma, or fear—can instill a false sense of isolation. This perceived separation disconnects individuals from their innate potential and creates a foundation for ego dominance.
   *Reflective Prompt:* Reflect on how early experiences of isolation might manifest in your clients. How might re-connecting with their inner spark foster healing?

7. **Everyone is divided by a psychological reality, creating the dimension of guilt and shame.**
   The division between one's authentic self and the defensive adaptations of the ego often results in feelings of guilt and shame. Most of us experience or label this **"life as it is."** These emotions further reinforce the illusion of separation. While guilt can motivate corrective actions, unresolved shame deeply affects one's self-image and perpetuates suffering.
   *Reflective Prompt:* In what ways do guilt and shame appear in your clinical observations? How might addressing these feelings pave the way for self-compassion?

8. **Everyone develops adaptive angst to cope with feelings of separation and division.**
   Adaptive angst is a response to the perceived break from one's true self—a division experienced either gradually as "death by a thousand splinters" or suddenly as "death by a stake to the heart." This angst drives the ego to adopt protective strategies, such as the critic, bully, mediator, or counselor lenses. Although these strategies help manage

pain, they often intensify suffering by reinforcing disconnection.
*Reflective Prompt:* Reflect on how adaptive angst might manifest in a client's behavior. How can you help them shift from ego-driven responses to more integrative approaches?

9. **Everyone must manage the emotional volatility relative to their ego's adaptations.**
The adaptive responses of the ego can result in significant emotional reactivity. Managing this volatility is crucial to accessing the heart's clarity. Techniques such as mindfulness and self-reflection are essential in regulating these intense emotional responses.
*Reflective Prompt:* How do you assist clients in regulating emotional volatility? Consider incorporating practices that promote self-regulation and mindfulness.

10. **Everyone's suffering offers the opportunity to discover their innate self-corrective design.**
Rather than viewing suffering solely as a negative experience, GCT interprets it as essential feedback—a signal prompting deeper self-awareness and growth. Every challenge holds the potential to reveal the hidden capacities for healing and alignment.
*Reflective Prompt:* Can you identify a case where suffering ultimately led to significant personal insight and growth? How might this perspective be shared with future clients?

**When individuals re-center the heart as the compass, their suffering decreases and they align with life as intended.** This final (**life as intended**) truth emphasizes that when the heart's wisdom guides one's actions, emotional clarity and balance emerge, reducing suffering and fostering a genuine connection with life.

*Reflective Prompt:* In what ways have you observed that clients who re-center their heart experience transformation? How does this re-centering affect their overall life satisfaction?

*Summary:*
Together, these 10 Absolute Truths form a comprehensive map of the human journey. They reveal that suffering is not a defect, but an integral part of growth—one that, when engaged with intentionally, opens the door to alignment and intentional evolution.

### 5.1.1 Progressive Insights—Evolved Outcomes from Alignment

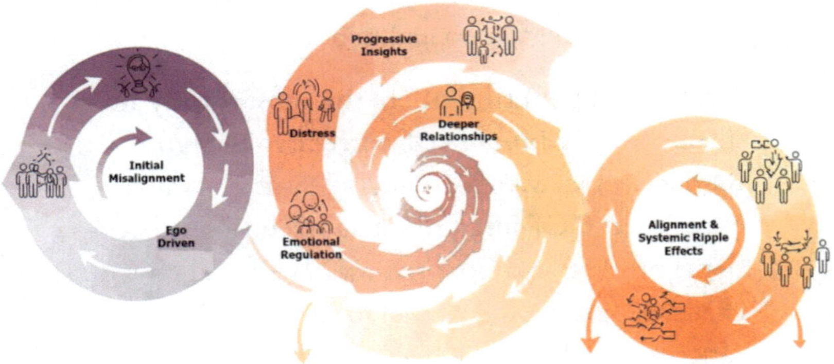


Embracing the 10 Absolute Truths marks the beginning of a transformative process. As individuals realign with their authentic nature, progressive insights naturally emerge. These insights represent the evolved outcomes of intentional evolution and manifest in several key areas:

- **Enhanced Emotional Regulation:**
  With alignment, clients report a reduction in emotional reactivity. Rather than being overwhelmed by transient feelings, they learn to process emotions calmly and constructively.
- **Deeper Interpersonal Relationships:**
  As the heart becomes the guiding compass, clients experience more authentic and reciprocal relationships. Communication improves, and connections are built on mutual respect and understanding.
- **Increased Resilience and Adaptability:**
  The aligned state strengthens an individual's capacity to bounce back from setbacks. This resilience is seen in the ability to navigate challenges with confidence and creative problem-solving.
- **Ripple Effects on Systemic Levels:**
  Research suggests that heart-centered living positively influences not only individual well-being but also relationships, community dynamics, and even organizational cultures (McCraty et al., 2015).

*Case Vignette:*
Consider a client who, after years of emotional turmoil, begins to embrace these truths. Over several months, their therapy sessions reveal marked improvements: they become less reactive, establish healthier boundaries in relationships, and report a newfound sense of purpose. These changes illustrate the progressive insights that naturally flow from alignment—a state of clarity, resilience, and interconnectedness.

**Reflective Prompt:**
Reflect on a breakthrough moment in your practice when a client's emotional regulation or relationship dynamics significantly improved. How did that shift manifest, and what progressive insights emerged?

*Additional Historical Context:*
These progressive insights echo both ancient wisdom and contemporary research. For instance, indigenous healing practices and Eastern philosophies have long emphasized the transformative power of aligning with one's inner truth—a perspective now supported by findings in neuroplasticity and emotional regulation.

*Summary:*
Progressive insights are the evolved outcomes that emerge when individuals align with their innate design. They are markers of transformation that not only enhance personal well-being but also have the potential to inspire systemic change.

### 5.1.2 When the 10 Absolutes Are Embraced

#### Insight #1: The Ego Must Surrender for the Heart to Lead

The journey toward alignment begins with the surrender of the ego's false dominance. Although the ego is adaptive, its overactivity—often a response to hurt, rejection, or trauma—creates resistance and perpetuates separation. GCT posits that true alignment occurs when the heart assumes its rightful role as the compass, integrating emotional, cognitive, and intuitive wisdom (Vecchio, 2025).

**The False Role of the Ego:**
The ego's need for control stems from fear—fear of vulnerability, failure, or uncertainty. This need often manifests as perfectionism, over analysis, or micromanagement, which may offer temporary relief but ultimately intensify suffering by reinforcing spiritual gravity.

*Example:*
A client who attempts to control every aspect of their life may experience heightened tension and burnout. Through GCT, they learn that relinquishing control allows the heart's clarity to emerge.

**Surrender as Humility and Trust:**
Surrendering the ego is an intentional process marked by humility and trust. By engaging the Observer and practicing self-compassion, clients learn to recognize the ego's distortions without judgment. This awareness creates space for the heart to guide decision-making, leading to more authentic choices.

*Clinical Application:*
Mindfulness exercises, reflective journaling, and guided imagery are effective strategies for cultivating this surrender. Over time, clients learn that trusting the heart not only alleviates stress but also deepens their connection to life.

**Reflective Prompt:**
How have you observed that letting go of control fosters greater clarity and authenticity in decision-making? Share a case where ego surrender led to transformational change.

### Insight #2: Humility as the Gateway to Transformation

Humility is the key that unlocks the psyche's self-corrective potential. In GCT, humility is not merely an admirable trait; it is essential for overcoming entrenched patterns and enabling the heart to lead. It allows individuals to confront their limitations, accept constructive feedback, and develop deeper self-awareness.

**Markers of Humility:**

- **Increased Self-Awareness:** Recognizing one's limitations without self-condemnation.
- **Openness to Feedback:** Embracing constructive criticism as an opportunity for growth.
- **Improved Interpersonal Dynamics:** Establishing healthier, more authentic relationships through reduced defensiveness.

*Example:*
A client with borderline personality disorder gradually learns to accept feedback, enabling them to better regulate their emotions and form healthier relationships. Over time, this humility becomes a catalyst for transformation.

**Reflective Prompt:**
How might fostering humility in your clients shift their patterns from self-criticism to self-growth?

### Insight #3: Compassion as Reciprocal Energy

GCT redefines compassion as a reciprocal energy—a dynamic flow of "suffering with" rather than "suffering for." Traditional views of compassion often place the burden solely on the caregiver, leading to over-responsibility and burnout. In contrast, GCT emphasizes mutual exchange, where both giver and receiver benefit from genuine, heart-led interaction.

**The Problem with "Suffering For":**
This perspective can lead to over-responsibility, martyrdom, and blurred boundaries that ultimately harm both parties.

**Reframing Compassion as "Suffering With":**
By engaging in compassion that is reciprocal, individuals experience balanced relationships where empathy flows freely without depleting either party.

*Example:*
A caregiver learns to set boundaries and practice self-compassion, which in turn enriches their relationships by fostering mutual respect and shared growth.

**Reflective Prompt:**
Reflect on how shifting from a self-sacrificial model of compassion to a reciprocal one might improve relational dynamics in your practice.

## Insight #4: Feelings as Present-Moment Gateways

GCT makes a pivotal distinction: feelings are immediate responses to the present, whereas emotions are re-enactments influenced by past narratives. Recognizing this difference allows clients to disconnect from reactive emotional loops and engage more fully with the present moment.

**Practical Application:**
Clients are taught to identify and name their feelings in real time without attaching past-based narratives. Mindfulness and journaling help separate transient feelings from entrenched emotional patterns.

*Example:*
A client learns to say, "I feel sad right now" without automatically defaulting to a narrative of chronic inadequacy, thereby reducing the intensity of their emotional reactivity.

**Reflective Prompt:**
How can differentiating between immediate feelings and past-triggered emotions enhance therapeutic outcomes in your sessions?

### Insight #5: Authenticity Emerges Naturally

Authenticity arises when the ego's distortions dissolve and the heart's guidance takes precedence. GCT posits that true authenticity is not manufactured—it is revealed when clients process guilt and shame and reconnect with their core essence.

**Differentiating Guilt and Shame:**

- **Guilt:** Serves as feedback that prompts corrective action.
- **Shame:** Deeply affects identity and requires profound healing to overcome.
  By addressing these emotions through self-compassion, clients can transform their vulnerabilities into strengths.

*Example:*
A client burdened by guilt learns to view their mistakes as opportunities for growth, allowing authenticity to emerge naturally over time.

**Reflective Prompt:**
In your experience, how does helping clients differentiate between guilt and shame facilitate deeper authenticity?

### Insight #6: Suffering Becomes Meaningful

GCT reframes suffering as a catalyst for transformation. Adversity tears down the ego's constructed character, creating an opportunity to rebuild from a place of alignment. Through intentional engagement with suffering, clients extract "salt" (wisdom) and "oil" (healing essence).

**The Transformative Process:**

- **Salt as Wisdom:** The distilled insights from adversity.
- **Oil as Healing Essence:** Self-compassion that lubricates the transition from resistance to alignment. This process turns adversity from a destructive force into a resource for growth.

**Reflective Prompt:**
How do you help clients reframe their experiences of suffering as opportunities for extracting wisdom and healing?

### Insight #7: Alignment Expands Systemically

Alignment cultivated through GCT does not remain confined to the individual; it extends outward to influence relationships, communities, and societal structures. When the heart leads, the clarity and compassion developed internally create ripple effects that inspire systemic transformation.

**The Individual as a Catalyst for Change**

- **Relational Transformation:**
  Aligned individuals foster authentic relationships characterized by empathy, trust, and mutual support.

- **Community Flourishment:**
  The ripple effect of personal alignment can enhance collective well-being and encourage collaborative action.

- **Organizational and Societal Impact:**
  Leaders who embody heart-centered values transform their organizations and contribute to broader systemic change.

*Example:*
A corporate leader who prioritizes employee well-being can foster a more humane organizational culture, leading to improved productivity and a sense of belonging among staff.

**Reflective Prompt:**
How have you seen individual alignment inspire positive changes in a community or organization? What small actions might you take to model this effect?

### Insight #8: Living the Humane Mandate—Life in a Humane Universe

Alignment through GCT ultimately culminates in living the "humane mandate"—a commitment to contribute compassionately and authentically to society. This mandate represents a bridge between personal healing and systemic transformation.

### Key Aspects of the Humane Mandate

- **Reciprocal Contribution:**
  Living the humane mandate involves balanced, reciprocal interactions that nourish both the individual and the community.

- **Compassionate Action:**
  Authentic, heart-led actions reduce suffering and promote collective well-being.
- **Systemic Influence:**
  When individuals live by the humane mandate, they serve as change agents, inspiring shifts toward more equitable and sustainable practices.

*Example:*
A community leader who champions access to mental health resources not only helps individuals but also paves the way for systemic reform that benefits society as a whole.

**Reflective Prompt:**
Consider how embracing the humane mandate might reshape your personal or professional life. What initiatives could you undertake to foster systemic change?

### Insight #9: Alignment Cultivates Synergistic Relationships

When individuals align with their heart, relationships evolve from transactional to synergistic—characterized by mutual growth, authenticity, and shared purpose.

#### Characteristics of Synergistic Relationships

1. **Authenticity:**
   True connection is fostered when individuals engage from a place of vulnerability and genuine self-expression.
2. **Shared Purpose:**
   Relationships rooted in common values and goals encourage collaborative growth.

3. **Resilience in Conflict:**
   Aligned individuals manage disagreements constructively, maintaining respect and empathy even in challenging situations.

*Example:*
A client who previously experienced one-sided, draining relationships begins to cultivate connections based on mutual support and shared purpose, transforming their relational dynamics.

**Reflective Prompt:**
How might fostering synergistic relationships alter the dynamics in your clients' personal or professional lives?

### Insight #10: Alignment as a Gateway to Universal Connection

At its deepest level, alignment transcends individual identity and dissolves the illusion of separation, fostering a profound sense of unity with all life. In this state, the boundaries between self and others become permeable, allowing for a dynamic, interconnected flow of energy.

**Universal Connection: Core Principles**

- **Transcending Egoic Isolation:**
  Alignment helps individuals overcome the false sense of isolation perpetuated by the ego.
- **Reciprocity and Stewardship:**
  Recognizing the interconnected nature of life fosters a sense of mutual responsibility.

- **Global Responsibility:**
  This insight expands personal alignment into a broader commitment to environmental, social, and global well-being.

*Example:*
A client who initially feels isolated may begin to participate in community service or environmental advocacy, discovering that their alignment contributes to a larger, collective effort.

**Reflective Prompt:**
How could a sense of universal connection influence the way you or your clients engage with the world? What actions might reflect this expanded perspective?

### 5.2 Integration and Synthesis

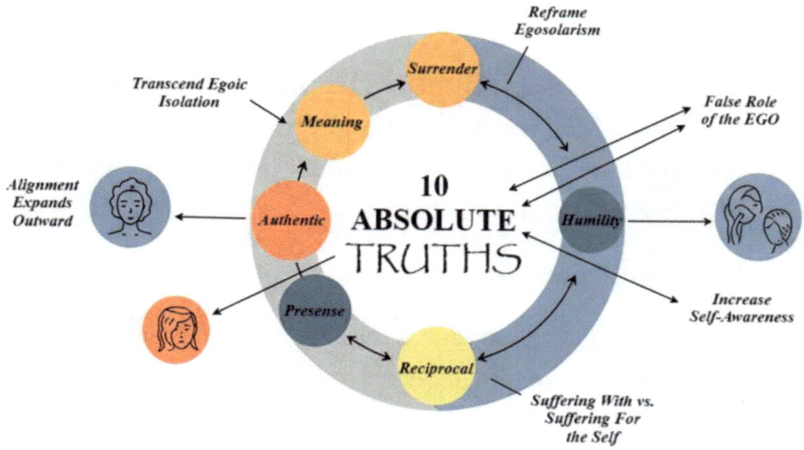


Bringing together the 10 Absolute Truths and the progressive insights creates a cohesive framework for intentional evolution. This synthesis demonstrates that every instance of misalignment offers the potential for growth when addressed with awareness and heart-centered practices.

**Integration of Elements:**

- The **Absolute Truths** provide a philosophical map of the human journey.
- **Progressive Insights** illustrate the evolved outcomes of alignment.
- The **Transformative Processes**—surrendering the ego, cultivating humility, redefining compassion—interact to reveal a unified, authentic self.

This integrative framework is not static but a dynamic process that evolves over time, encouraging continual reflection and growth. It serves as the foundation for both individual transformation and systemic change, as aligned individuals naturally radiate their inner clarity outward into their communities.

**Reflective Prompt:**
How do the various elements of GCT's framework interconnect in your practice? Identify one key insight from this synthesis that you find most transformative and consider how it might guide your next therapeutic intervention.

**Conclusion and Transitional Note**

Diagnostic tools and the practical framework of Gifted Compassionate Therapy have been presented as a comprehensive, integrative roadmap for alignment. The 10 Absolute Truths, progressive insights, and the subsequent transformative processes collectively guide individuals from fragmentation to intentional evolution. This chapter has provided a robust framework for understanding how personal suffering can be transformed into wisdom and healing—a journey that culminates in authentic, heart-centered living.

## Final Integration: Practical Applications and Future Directions

### Detailed Session Protocols and Intervention Outlines

To illustrate the practical application of these concepts, consider the following sample therapy session outline designed for GCT:

1. **Mindful Check-In and Observer Activation (15 minutes):**
    - Begin with a guided mindfulness exercise (e.g., breathing meditation) to help clients center themselves and activate the Observer.
    - Use reflective prompts such as, "What sensations are you noticing right now?"
2. **Exploration of the 10 Absolute Truths (20 minutes):**
    - Discuss one or two of the Absolute Truths, relating them to the client's personal experience.
    - Invite the client to share memories where they felt either aligned with or separated from their inner spark.
    - Use questions like, "Can you recall a time when you felt a deep, unfiltered connection to life?"
3. **Progressive Insights and Suffering Reframing (25 minutes):**
    - Engage the client in a narrative exercise where they reframe recent challenges in terms of the progressive insights (e.g., transforming adaptive angst into growth opportunities).

- Encourage journaling or drawing as a means of expressing how their suffering might be transformed into "salt" and "oil."

4. **Action Planning and Integration (20 minutes):**
    - Collaboratively develop a plan for integrating these insights into daily life.
    - Set small, measurable goals (e.g., practicing self-compassion exercises, engaging in community activities) that align with the humane mandate.
    - Conclude by discussing how these actions might ripple out into improved relationships and community engagement.

*Reflective Prompt:*
How might you adapt this session outline for different client needs? Consider modifications for individual versus group settings, and how you might incorporate additional modalities (such as art therapy or movement) to further reinforce these principles.

**Group and Community Applications**

In addition to individual therapy, GCT's framework can be extended to group and community contexts:

- **Workshops and Support Groups:**
  Design sessions focused on the 10 Absolute Truths, using guided group discussions, role-playing, and collaborative exercises to help participants explore shared experiences and foster collective alignment.

- **Community Initiatives:**
  Develop community projects (such as neighborhood gardens or local art programs) that embody the principles of reciprocal compassion and universal connection. Such initiatives not only benefit participants but also demonstrate the systemic impact of alignment.

- **Organizational Interventions:**
  In workplaces, implement training programs that promote heart-centered leadership and collaborative practices, thereby enhancing organizational culture and employee well-being (Boyatzis et al., 2002).

**Future Research and Systemic Implications**

The framework of GCT is not static. Ongoing research in neuroplasticity, heart coherence, and trauma-informed care continues to refine our understanding of the self-corrective capacities of the human psyche. Future studies may further validate the impact of intentional evolution on both individual healing and systemic transformation. For example:

- **Longitudinal Studies:**
  Research tracking clients over several years can help establish the durability of alignment and its effects on quality of life.

- **Neuroimaging Studies:**
  Investigations into brain-heart interactions may provide empirical evidence supporting the claims of heart-centered healing.

- **Cross-Cultural Research:**
  Comparative studies across cultures could elucidate how

universal the 10 Absolute Truths are and how they might be adapted for diverse populations.

*Reflective Prompt:*
What areas of research do you believe are most critical for further validating GCT's approach? How might emerging studies influence your clinical practice?

**Integration and Synthesis Recap**

To synthesize, the practical framework of GCT is built upon a foundation of universal truths and progressive insights that together form a roadmap for intentional evolution. The 10 Absolute Truths chart the developmental journey of the human psyche, while the progressive insights reveal the transformative potential of alignment. Through clinical interventions, reflective practices, and systemic applications, GCT empowers individuals to re-center their hearts and live authentically, thus creating a ripple effect that extends into their communities and beyond.

*Final Reflective Prompt:*
In your own words, what is the most transformative insight from this framework? How would you communicate this to a client in a way that inspires hope and action?

**5.3 Navigating Client Resistance to GCT Concepts**

While the 10 Absolute Truths offer a profound framework for transformation, therapists will inevitably encounter resistance when introducing these concepts to clients. This resistance is not merely an obstacle to overcome but valuable information about the client's relationship to their ego structures and heart disconnection. By skillfully addressing these points of resistance, therapists can deepen the therapeutic process and facilitate more authentic engagement with GCT principles.

## Common Forms of Client Resistance

### Intellectual Skepticism

Many clients, particularly those with strong left-brain dominance or academic backgrounds, may challenge GCT concepts as unscientific or overly metaphorical. This skepticism often manifests as:

- Requests for empirical evidence or research studies
- Dismissal of concepts like "heart as compass" as merely symbolic
- Intellectualization that keeps concepts at arm's length
- Comparison to other therapeutic approaches they consider more "legitimate"

### Ego Protection

Since GCT directly addresses ego dysfunction, the ego naturally mounts resistance to protect its centrality:

- Deflection through focusing on external problems rather than internal patterns
- Urgent problem-solving that bypasses deeper alignment work
- Impatience with observer activation exercises ("This isn't fixing anything")
- Reframing therapeutic insights as already known ("I already knew that")

**Spiritual Bypass Tendencies**

Some clients with spiritual backgrounds may attempt to use GCT concepts to bypass necessary emotional processing:

- Premature forgiveness before fully processing hurt
- Abstract philosophical discussions that avoid personal application
- Using "heart-centered" language without embodied integration
- Resistance to acknowledging painful emotions in favor of "positivity"

**Fear of Vulnerability**

Many clients fear the vulnerability that comes with heart reconnection:

- Concern that compassion equals weakness
- Worry that releasing ego control will lead to harm or exploitation
- Reluctance to feel previously suppressed emotions
- Fear that authenticity will damage important relationships

**Strategies for Addressing Resistance**

**For Intellectual Skepticism:**

1. **Meet clients where they are** by connecting GCT concepts to established research in neuroscience, polyvagal theory, and psychophysiology. *Example Dialogue:* **Client:** "This heart as compass idea seems nice, but it's just a metaphor, not something real." **Therapist:** "I

appreciate your critical thinking. What we're calling the 'heart as compass' is actually supported by research from the HeartMath Institute showing that the heart contains neural cells that process information independently from the brain. When I mention the heart's wisdom, I'm referring to this documented physiological system, not just a poetic idea."

2. **Offer experiential evidence** alongside intellectual explanations. *Example Dialogue:* **Client:** "I need evidence that this approach actually works." **Therapist:** "That makes sense. While I can share research studies, the most compelling evidence often comes from direct experience. Would you be willing to try a brief exercise so you can evaluate the impact for yourself?"
3. **Validate the protective function** of intellectual questioning while gently inviting deeper exploration. *Example Dialogue:* **Client:** "I've read about these concepts before, and they're interesting theoretically, but I'm not sure they apply to real problems." **Therapist:** "Your analytical mind has clearly helped you navigate complex ideas, which is a strength. I wonder if we might explore how these concepts might apply specifically to your situation, not just theoretically. Would you be open to that kind of exploration alongside the intellectual understanding?"

**For Ego Protection:**

1. **Acknowledge the ego's adaptive function** before suggesting alternatives. *Example Dialogue:* **Client:** "I don't see why I need to 'observe my thoughts.' I need to solve this problem with my boss." **Therapist:** "Your focus on

finding concrete solutions has likely served you well in many situations. That problem-solving capacity is valuable. Observer activation isn't about replacing that skill—it's about adding another dimension that might reveal options your problem-solving mind hasn't considered yet."

2. **Use gentle humor** to create perspective on ego patterns. *Example Dialogue:* **Client:** "This inner critic you keep mentioning—it's just being realistic about my flaws." **Therapist:** "The critic is quite convincing, isn't it? It's like having a very serious internal commentator who's absolutely certain they're just reporting facts. What if we got a little curious about whether this commentator might be a bit dramatic sometimes?"

3. **Demonstrate rather than explain** by modeling observer awareness in session. *Example Dialogue:* **Client:** "I don't understand all this observer talk. It seems abstract." **Therapist:** "I notice right now that as we're talking, I'm feeling a tightness in my chest and an urge to convince you. That's my ego wanting to prove something. If I step back and observe that reaction rather than acting from it, I can respond more openly. That's the observer in action. Did you notice the shift in our interaction just now?"

**For Spiritual Bypass Tendencies:**

1. **Distinguish between true heart alignment and premature transcendence.** *Example Dialogue:* **Client:** "I know I should forgive my father because holding onto anger isn't spiritual." **Therapist:** "True heart-centered forgiveness actually embraces the full range of emotions first, including the anger. The heart doesn't ask us to

bypass difficult feelings—it helps us move through them authentically. What might your heart need before forgiveness feels genuine rather than obligatory?"

2. **Ground spiritual concepts in embodied experience.** *Example Dialogue:* **Client:** "I understand conceptually that we're all connected at a spiritual level." **Therapist:** "I'm curious—where do you feel that connection in your body when it's a lived experience rather than a concept? Can you recall a moment when you felt that connection directly, not just thought about it?"

3. **Honor spiritual language while deepening emotional resonance.** *Example Dialogue:* **Client:** "I know I should practice compassion toward my ex-partner." **Therapist:** "I hear your commitment to compassion, which is beautiful. I'm wondering what happens in your body when you think about extending compassion to your ex-partner? Does it feel expansive and natural, or is there some contraction that might need acknowledgment first?"

**For Fear of Vulnerability:**

1. **Create safety through clear boundaries and titrated exposure.** *Example Dialogue:* **Client:** "If I start feeling all these emotions, I'll fall apart completely." **Therapist:** "That concern makes perfect sense. Our approach will be gradual and contained. You'll always have the ability to pause or step back if things feel overwhelming. Would it be helpful to establish a clear signal you can use if you need to take a break from emotional exploration?"

2. **Reframe vulnerability as strength** through concrete examples. *Example Dialogue:* **Client:** "Being heart-centered sounds nice, but in the real world, people will take

advantage of you." **Therapist:** "That's an important concern. Heart-centered living isn't about removing all boundaries—in fact, it often leads to clearer, stronger boundaries because they're based on authentic values rather than fear. Nelson Mandela and Martin Luther King Jr. exemplified this heart-centered strength. Their vulnerability wasn't weakness—it was the source of their transformative impact."

3. **Use gradual exposure** to build confidence in heart-centered responses. *Example Dialogue:* **Client:** "I can't imagine being vulnerable with my family after all that's happened." **Therapist:** "Complete vulnerability immediately would be overwhelming. What if we started with small moments of authenticity in lower-risk situations? Perhaps practicing with a trusted friend first, or even in our sessions, to build your confidence in this approach before applying it in more challenging relationships."

**Resistance as Information: The Diagnostic Value of Client Challenges**

Client resistance provides valuable diagnostic information about:

1. **Dominant Ego Lens:** The specific nature of resistance often reveals which ego lens is most active.
   - Critic lens: "I'm not doing this heart-centered thing correctly."
   - Bully lens: "This approach is too soft; it won't work in the real world."

- Mediator lens: "I understand the concept, but my family would never accept me being authentic."
- Counselor lens: "I need to understand the theoretical basis before I can apply this."

2. **Developmental Trauma Points:** Resistance typically emerges most strongly around areas of unresolved developmental wounds.
3. **Window of Tolerance:** The intensity of resistance indicates how much integration work is needed before introducing more challenging concepts.

**Case Example: Working Through Resistance to Observer Activation**

**Client Background:** Michael, a 42-year-old attorney, entered therapy for anxiety and relationship difficulties. Highly analytical and achievement-oriented, he initially viewed the observer concept with substantial skepticism.

**Initial Resistance:** "This observer idea sounds like dissociation to me. I need practical tools, not meditation techniques."

**Therapeutic Approach:**

1. **Meeting intellectual needs:** The therapist provided neurobiological research on metacognition and explained how observer activation differs from dissociation by increasing integration rather than separation.
2. **Offering experiential evidence:** The therapist guided Michael through a brief observer exercise focused on his physical sensations during a discussion of a work conflict.

3. **Connecting to valued outcomes:** The therapist linked observer activation to Michael's stated goals of reducing reactivity in high-stakes negotiations.

**Breakthrough Moment:** After several sessions of gradual exposure to observer practices, Michael reported a significant insight: "During court yesterday, I noticed my heart racing and thoughts spiraling about the judge's reactions. Instead of getting hijacked by that anxiety, I was able to observe it and stay focused on my argument. It was a completely different experience."

**Integration:** Over time, Michael began initiating observer activation on his own, reporting improved emotional regulation and more satisfying interactions with colleagues and family members.

### Ethical Considerations in Addressing Resistance

While working with resistance is essential, therapists must maintain ethical boundaries:

1. **Respect client autonomy:** If a client decisively rejects certain GCT concepts after thoughtful exploration, respect their decision rather than pushing for acceptance.
2. **Avoid spiritual imposition:** Present GCT concepts in language that respects the client's worldview, whether secular, religious, or spiritual.
3. **Maintain appropriate pacing:** Some resistance indicates that the therapeutic process is moving too quickly. Adjust accordingly.
4. **Practice self-awareness:** Differentiate between genuine client resistance and your own agenda for the client's growth.

**Resistance as Opportunity**

When approached with curiosity and compassion, resistance becomes not an obstacle but a gateway to deeper therapeutic work. By honoring the protective function of resistance while gently inviting exploration beyond it, therapists can help clients experience the transformative potential of the 10 Absolute Truths. Each point of resistance, skillfully navigated, becomes an opportunity for the client to experience the very shift from ego-centered to heart-centered awareness that lies at the core of GCT.

**Conclusion and Transitional Note**

In this chapter, we have outlined the comprehensive practical framework for Gifted Compassionate Therapy. By presenting the 10 Absolute Truths, exploring progressive insights, and detailing actionable interventions, we have constructed a robust model that transforms individual suffering into an opportunity for growth and systemic change. This framework not only challenges conventional therapeutic paradigms but also provides integrative therapists with a rich, multidimensional roadmap for fostering alignment and inte The practical framework of GCT, anchored in the 10 Absolute Truths and progressive insights, offers a comprehensive roadmap for guiding clients from ego-driven suffering to heart-centered alignment. These truths and insights are not isolated concepts—they form an integrated system that addresses the whole person and facilitates intentional evolution through systematic, compassionate intervention.

Having established this foundation, we now explore how GCT integrates with and enhances existing psychotherapeutic approaches. Chapter Seven demonstrates that GCT is not meant to replace traditional therapeutic models, but rather to provide an overarching framework that enriches them. By understanding how approaches such as CBT, DBT, IFS, somatic therapy, and psychodynamic and most other models can be viewed through the lens of GCT, therapists can leverage familiar techniques while simultaneously addressing deeper misalignments.

This integration is essential because most clinicians have already developed expertise in specific modalities. The question is not whether to abandon these approaches, but how to infuse them with GCT's heart-centered perspective, thereby expanding their transformative potential. As we examine each model through the GCT framework, consider how your existing therapeutic skills might be enhanced by re-centering the heart as the compass of healing and intentional evolution.

# Chapter Seven
# Integration of Psychotherapeutic Models

## Introduction

The field of psychotherapy offers a rich tapestry of models and approaches, each contributing unique insights into human behavior and healing. Traditional therapies tend to focus on specific dimensions—whether cognitive, emotional, relational, or somatic—but Gifted Compassionate Therapy (GCT) seeks to integrate and transcend these perspectives by addressing the whole self. GCT provides a unifying framework that acknowledges the interdependence of the observer, spirit, ego, and heart, aligning them with the psyche's inherent capacity for self-correction and growth.

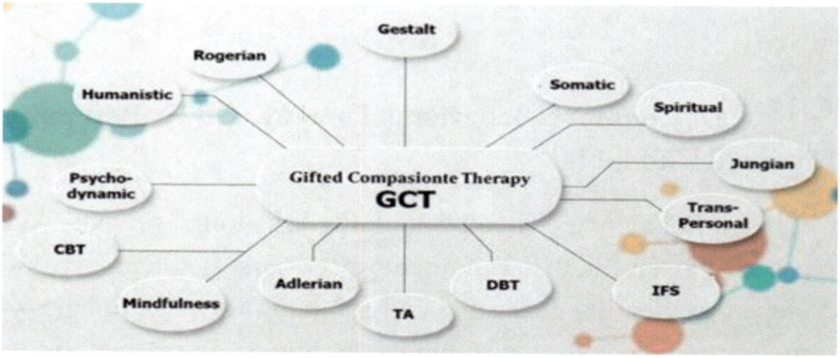

At its core, GCT does not reject established therapeutic models; rather, it synthesizes their foundational principles with its own emphasis on humane alignment, intentional evolution, and the heart as the true compass. In doing so, GCT bridges the divide between approaches such as Cognitive-Behavioral Therapy (CBT), Dialectical Behavior Therapy (DBT), Internal Family Systems (IFS), somatic therapy, and psychodynamic therapy. It also addresses complex issues such as ego dysfunction and narcissistic personality traits. This chapter illustrates how GCT can complement and enhance these established models by:

- Outlining their core principles,
- Demonstrating natural integration with GCT's philosophy, and
- Presenting practical applications and case examples that reveal the synergy between these modalities.

By weaving together these diverse perspectives, GCT expands the capacity for healing beyond mere symptom management. It offers a pathway to rediscover life as it was intended—through intentional evolution, where suffering is seen as a signal for realignment rather than a defect to be fixed.

## 6.1 Cognitive-Behavioral Therapy (CBT): Reframing Distorted Thoughts

Cognitive-Behavioral Therapy (CBT) has long served as a cornerstone of modern psychotherapy. Its structured framework—designed to identify, challenge, and reframe distorted thoughts—rests on the principle that thoughts, emotions, and behaviors are interconnected (Beck, 1976). CBT provides practical tools to interrupt cycles of negative thinking and maladaptive behaviors. GCT naturally complements CBT by broadening its focus to include the heart's role in restoring alignment and reducing suffering (Vecchio, 2025).

**Core Principles of CBT**

1. **Cognitive Distortions:**
   CBT helps clients identify and reframe unhelpful thought patterns that drive emotional distress (Clark & Beck, 2010).

2. **Behavioral Activation:**
   It encourages clients to engage in proactive behaviors to counteract avoidance and promote full engagement with life (Jacobson et al., 2001).

3. **Thought-Emotion-Behavior Connection:**
   The therapy emphasizes that the interplay between thoughts, emotions, and behaviors significantly affects mental health (Beck, 1976).

While CBT focuses primarily on rational analysis and behavior modification, its approach may sometimes overlook the deeper emotional and intuitive wisdom housed within the heart (Vecchio, 2025). GCT integrates the observer and heart to complement CBT's methods, enriching the process of reframing cognitive distortions.

**Integration of GCT with CBT**

1. **The Observer in Cognitive Awareness:**
   CBT teaches clients to recognize distorted thoughts through self-monitoring. GCT enhances this process by activating the observer—a neutral, nonjudgmental witness

that sees these distortions without attachment. This added layer of awareness allows clients to distance themselves from ego-driven narratives (Clark & Beck, 2010; Vecchio, 2025).
*Example:*
A client tormented by the thought, "I'm a failure," may initially counter this belief by gathering evidence of past successes. With GCT, the client also learns to notice that this thought is rooted in the critic lens of the ego, thereby inviting the observer to detach from the reaction.

2. **Compassionate Reframing through the Heart:**
Rather than solely relying on rational counterarguments, GCT encourages clients to reframe thoughts by engaging the heart's compassionate perspective. This method shifts the focus from merely proving a thought wrong to understanding the emotional wound that underlies it (Vecchio, 2025).
*Example:*
Instead of merely countering "I'm a failure" with "I've succeeded before," the client is guided to reframe the thought compassionately: "Even though I feel like a failure, I am worthy of care and growth."

3. **Beyond Symptom Management:**
CBT's strength lies in reducing symptoms through thought and behavior modification. GCT expands this aim by also re-centering the heart as the internal compass, thus fostering intentional evolution and a deeper sense of purpose (Vecchio, 2025).
*Example:*
A client with social anxiety might use CBT to gradually reengage in social situations, while GCT encourages an

exploration of past wounds (such as rejection) that distort their ego's perception, ultimately enabling a more authentic reengagement.

**Practical Applications:**

- **Thought Records with Observer Activation:**
  Traditional CBT thought records are adapted to include the observer's perspective. Clients not only list their thoughts but also identify which egoic lens (e.g., critic) is active, and then use the heart to reframe the thought.
  *Sample Thought Record:*
    - **Situation:** "I missed a work deadline."
    - **Thought:** "I'm incompetent."
    - **Observer Insight:** "This thought is driven by my critic lens; it is a distortion."
    - **Heart Reframe:** "Mistakes are human; I can learn and improve without my worth being diminished."
- **Behavioral Experiments with Heart-Centered Reflection:**
  Clients test out new behaviors while pausing afterward to reflect on how their heart perceives the outcomes. This process adds depth to traditional CBT experiments and reinforces alignment.

*Reflective Prompt:*
How can integrating the observer and heart's perspective into CBT techniques enhance your clients' ability to reframe distorted thoughts? What additional exercises might you implement?

While Cognitive-Behavioral Therapy provides valuable tools for restructuring distorted thoughts and modifying behaviors, it sometimes falls short in addressing the intense emotional dysregulation that many clients experience. This is where Dialectical Behavior Therapy (DBT) extends the cognitive-behavioral framework by emphasizing the balance between acceptance and change—a dialectic that mirrors GCT's own balance between acknowledging present realities while facilitating intentional evolution. As we shift our focus to DBT, notice how its emphasis on mindfulness and emotional regulation naturally complements GCT's observer activation and heart-centered awareness. Both approaches recognize that transformation requires not just cognitive change but also the capacity to remain present with difficult emotions without being overwhelmed by them.

## 6.2 Dialectical Behavior Therapy (DBT): Emotional Regulation and Mindfulness

Dialectical Behavior Therapy (DBT) is a structured, evidence-based approach designed to help individuals regulate their emotions, improve interpersonal effectiveness, tolerate distress, and cultivate mindfulness (Linehan, 1993). Its emphasis on balancing acceptance with change aligns naturally with GCT's philosophy of intentional evolution and heart-centered alignment (Vecchio, 2025).

### Core Principles of DBT

1. **Mindfulness:**
   Developing an awareness of the present moment while observing thoughts and emotions nonjudgmentally (Linehan, 2015).

2. **Distress Tolerance:**
   Building skills to cope with and accept difficult emotions without engaging in reactive behaviors (Linehan, 1993).

3. **Emotion Regulation:**
   Gaining insight into and managing intense emotional experiences (Linehan, 2015).

4. **Interpersonal Effectiveness:**
   Enhancing communication and boundary-setting skills to foster healthier relationships (Linehan, 1993).

**Integration of GCT with DBT**

GCT enriches DBT by introducing the heart as the central guide for emotional clarity and the observer as a stabilizing force in mindfulness practice.

1. **The Observer as the Anchor:**
   DBT's mindfulness practices are deepened by engaging the observer, which helps clients remain neutrally aware of their internal experiences. This additional layer of neutrality enables a clearer separation from ego-driven reactivity (Vecchio, 2025).

2. **The Heart in Emotional Regulation:**
   While DBT employs techniques such as opposite action and self-soothing, GCT integrates the heart's compassionate guidance to help reframe emotional experiences. The result is not only a reduction in distress but also a deeper realignment with personal values and purpose.

*Reflective Prompt:*
How might incorporating the observer and heart-centered

practices into DBT interventions enhance emotional regulation in your clients? What changes could this integration bring to their interpersonal relationships?

The skills-based approach of DBT helps clients build specific competencies for emotional regulation and interpersonal effectiveness, yet some clients need a deeper understanding of the internal dynamics driving their reactions. Internal Family Systems (IFS) takes us into this inner landscape by viewing the psyche as a constellation of parts rather than a monolithic entity. This perspective beautifully complements GCT's understanding of the egoic lenses—critic, bully, mediator, and counselor—as distinct aspects of self that have developed for protective purposes. Both IFS and GCT recognize that true healing emerges not from battling these parts but from understanding their intentions and integrating them into a more cohesive whole guided by a compassionate center.

### 6.3 Internal Family Systems (IFS): Integration of Ego States

Internal Family Systems (IFS), developed by Dr. Richard Schwartz, views the psyche as a constellation of parts—each with its own emotions, beliefs, and roles. IFS emphasizes the process of unblending these parts and reconnecting them with the Self—a core state of calm, clarity, and compassion (Schwartz, 1995). GCT aligns seamlessly with IFS by mapping the ego's four lenses (critic, bully, mediator, counselor) and highlighting the heart's role as the true compass.

## Core Principles of IFS

1. **Multiplicity of the Psyche:**
   The mind comprises distinct parts, including protectors and exiles (Schwartz, 1995).

2. **The Self as Leader:**
   The Self represents the calm, clear center that guides healing and integration (Schwartz, 2021).

3. **Unblending and Healing:**
   Clients learn to "unblend" from reactive parts, observing them with curiosity and compassion.

## Integration of GCT with IFS

GCT deepens IFS work by connecting egoic parts to the broader framework of the observer, spirit, ego, and heart. This integration enhances the process of unblending and fosters alignment through the heart's compassionate guidance.

1. **The Observer and Unblending:**
   IFS encourages clients to unblend from reactive parts by observing them nonjudgmentally. GCT supplements this process by activating the observer as a unifying presence that helps identify which egoic lens (e.g., critic or bully) is active, thereby reducing emotional reactivity (Vecchio, 2025).

2. **Heart-Centered Reparenting:**
   IFS recognizes that healing occurs when vulnerable parts feel safe. GCT adds that the heart's compassion is essential in reparenting these parts, transforming painful memories into opportunities for growth.

3. **Mapping Egoic Lenses:**
   GCT reframes the protective parts identified in IFS as egoic lenses. By understanding these lenses and their origins, clients can work toward realigning their behavior with heart-led authenticity.

*Clinical Example:*
Rachel, a 42-year-old teacher with anxiety and perfectionism, learns through IFS that her inner critic (a protective part) is trying to shield her from rejection. GCT guides her to activate her observer and reframe the critic's voice from a source of self-condemnation to a signal for deeper self-care.

*Reflective Prompt:*
How might the integration of IFS and GCT provide a more holistic view of a client's internal dynamics? In what ways does the heart's perspective change the interpretation of egoic parts?

While IFS provides profound insight into the internal system of parts, its focus can sometimes remain primarily cognitive and emotional. Yet, as GCT recognizes, human experience is fundamentally embodied—our traumas, defenses, and healing processes all have physiological dimensions. Somatic therapy addresses this dimension directly, acknowledging that the body holds what the conscious mind cannot always access. This somatic perspective enriches GCT's framework by providing concrete methods to address the physical manifestations of spiritual gravity and ego distortion. As we explore somatic approaches, notice how they complement the observer activation and heart-centering techniques of GCT by anchoring awareness in the body's wisdom.

SOMATIC

## 6.4 Somatic Therapy: Addressing Embodied Trauma and Tension

Somatic therapy is founded on the recognition that trauma and emotional experiences are stored in the body as physical sensations and tension. This modality emphasizes the body-mind connection and utilizes techniques such as body awareness, movement, and breathwork to facilitate healing (Levine, 1997; van der Kolk, 2014). GCT complements somatic therapy by integrating the observer's neutrality and the heart's guidance into the process of releasing embodied trauma.

### Core Principles of Somatic Therapy

1. **The Body as a Repository:**
   Traumatic experiences and emotional pain are often held in the body as tension or discomfort.
2. **Embodied Awareness:**
   Cultivating awareness of bodily sensations in the present moment allows clients to access and release stored trauma.
3. **Restoring Regulation:**
   Techniques that restore the body's natural self-regulation (through parasympathetic activation) are crucial for healing.

### Integration of GCT with Somatic Therapy

1. **Activating the Observer:**
   In somatic practices, clients learn to observe bodily sensations without judgment. GCT enhances this by emphasizing the role of the observer to notice sensations, emotions, and their corresponding egoic responses, thereby fostering detachment from reactive patterns.

2. **The Heart's Role in Healing:**
   GCT integrates heart-centered reflection into somatic work. For example, during a body scan, clients may be guided to connect with the warmth of the heart as they notice areas of tension, thereby inviting a compassionate response that aids in releasing trauma.
3. **Releasing Egoic Patterns:**
   Physical tension can reflect specific egoic lenses at work. GCT helps clients identify and reframe these patterns, such as recognizing that chronic shoulder tension may be associated with a protective mediator lens that overcompensates for emotional overwhelm.

*Practical Application:*
A session might involve a guided body scan where the client notices tension in their stomach. The therapist invites the client to engage their observer, noting the sensation without judgment, and then to bring gentle attention to the heart, visualizing the breath flowing in and out of that region.

*Reflective Prompt:*
How can you incorporate somatic practices into your therapeutic sessions to help clients connect with their heart's wisdom? What additional movement or breathwork exercises might complement this approach?

Somatic approaches illuminate the body's role in both holding distress and facilitating healing, yet they may not fully address the historical and unconscious dimensions of the psyche. Psychodynamic therapy enriches our understanding by exploring how early experiences and unconscious patterns shape current functioning. This historical depth complements GCT's recognition that ego patterns often originate in childhood adaptations that once served important protective functions. Both approaches acknowledge that true transformation requires not just present-moment awareness but also an understanding of the developmental journey that shaped our current patterns. By integrating psychodynamic insights with GCT's framework, we gain a more complete picture of how the past influences the present and how healing can unfold across time.

While psychodynamic approaches excel at illuminating the origins and unconscious dynamics of psychological patterns, they sometimes struggle to address more severe forms of ego dysfunction, particularly conditions like narcissistic personality traits that resist traditional insight-oriented methods. GCT offers unique perspectives on these challenging presentations by directly addressing the fundamental misalignment at their core—the exaggerated ego functioning that has displaced the heart as the guiding compass. As we turn to examining ego dysfunction through the GCT lens, notice how the principles we've explored in other modalities converge to address one of the most difficult challenges in clinical practice: working with clients whose ego defenses resist conventional therapeutic approaches.

Freud
Psychodynamic

## 6.5 Psychodynamic Therapy: Exploring the Unconscious and Relational Patterns

Psychodynamic therapy holds that unconscious processes, early experiences, and relational dynamics profoundly shape behavior, thoughts, and emotions (Freud, 1917/1957; Shedler, 2010). It emphasizes uncovering these hidden influences and exploring their impact on current functioning. GCT enriches psychodynamic therapy by integrating the observer, heart, ego, and spirit into this exploration—offering tools for recognizing egoic distortions and aligning with deeper emotional truths.

**Core Principles of Psychodynamic Therapy**

1. **Unconscious Influences:**
   Unresolved conflicts and early life experiences continue to shape present behavior.

2. **Attachment and Early Relationships:**
   Internalized relational patterns from childhood influence adult relationships.

3. **Transference and Countertransference:**
   The therapeutic relationship mirrors unconscious dynamics, offering a space for insight and change.

4. **Insight and Emotional Expression:**
   Healing arises from understanding and expressing previously repressed emotions.

**Integration of GCT with Psychodynamic Therapy**

1. **The Observer's Role:**
   GCT introduces the observer as a means to view unconscious patterns without judgment. This helps clients recognize defensive reactions and transference phenomena more objectively, facilitating deeper insight.

2. **The Heart's Compassion in Healing:**
   By bringing the heart into the therapeutic process, GCT encourages clients to reframe painful attachment wounds with self-compassion. This shift allows clients to process early relational trauma in a nurturing environment.

3. **Mapping Defense Mechanisms:**
   GCT's identification of egoic lenses complements psychodynamic work by pinpointing which defense mechanisms (e.g., repression, projection) are at play.

Clients learn to attribute these patterns to specific ego functions, which can then be gently realigned with the heart's guidance.

*Case Example:*
Eric, a 34-year-old engineer, struggles with intimacy due to childhood experiences of emotional neglect. Traditional psychodynamic therapy helps him uncover these patterns, while GCT further guides him to use the observer to notice how his ego's critic lens distorts his self-perception. By engaging his heart's compassion, Eric begins to reframe his experiences, paving the way for healthier relational patterns.

*Reflective Prompt:*
How might you use the observer and heart frameworks to enrich psychodynamic exploration in your sessions? What specific interventions could help clients bridge the gap between unconscious patterns and conscious healing?

## 6.6 Ego Dysfunction and Narcissistic Personality Traits: How GCT Addresses the Issue

Personality disorders—particularly Narcissistic Personality Disorder (NPD) and other Cluster B conditions—are challenging expressions of ego dysfunction. Traditional therapeutic models often struggle to engage individuals with narcissistic traits, as these clients typically resist introspection, externalize blame, and exhibit low emotional receptivity (American Psychiatric Association, 2013). GCT offers a unique framework that addresses these ego distortions by re-centering the heart and reducing the pull of spiritual gravity.

### Prevalence and Impact

Research suggests that narcissistic traits exist on a continuum. Although only a fraction of individuals meet the clinical criteria for NPD, studies estimate that approximately 6.2% of the U.S. population reports lifetime NPD traits (Stinson et al., 2008), with a notable gender difference favoring higher prevalence in men. Moreover, narcissistic dysfunction often co-occurs with other disorders such as substance use, mood and anxiety disorders, complicating treatment further (Grant et al., 2008).

### Impact on Relationships and Systems

Narcissistic dysfunction does not occur in isolation; its effects ripple through personal relationships and social systems. For instance, research by Brown (2015) indicates that millions of individuals are indirectly affected by narcissistic relational dynamics, leading to widespread interpersonal distress and systemic dysfunction.

### How GCT Addresses Ego Dysfunction

1. **Disrupting Ego Solarism:**
   GCT bypasses the narcissistic defense mechanisms by engaging the observer to identify ego distortions and guiding clients to realign with the heart's wisdom (Vecchio, 2025). This process diminishes the ego's false sense of centrality.

2. **Shifting Compassion from Self-Serving to Reciprocal:**
   GCT reframes compassion from "suffering for" (which often reinforces narcissistic self-importance) to "suffering with," encouraging balanced, reciprocal relationships that promote mutual growth (Vecchio, 2025).

3. **Addressing the Guilt-Shame Split:**
   Narcissistic dysfunction often involves an unresolved split between guilt and shame. GCT helps clients reframe guilt as a signal for growth and shame as an opportunity for healing—both of which require a strong connection to the heart.

4. **Supporting Survivors of Narcissistic Abuse:**
   GCT not only addresses narcissistic traits in clients but also provides a recovery path for those affected by narcissistic relationships, helping survivors rebuild self-care, regain autonomy, and break destructive cycles (Brown, 2015).

*Reflective Prompt:*
How could you adapt interventions to help clients with narcissistic traits move beyond ego-driven defenses and towards heart-centered alignment? What are some practical steps to foster reciprocal compassion in these cases?

*Summary:*
By addressing the core elements of ego dysfunction—ego solarism, the guilt-shame split, and self-serving compassion—GCT offers a transformative approach that benefits both clients with narcissistic traits and those affected by them.

The patterns of ego dysfunction we've explored represent extreme manifestations of ego-solarism, yet they also reveal the universal human struggle with identity and authenticity. Jungian psychology deepens our understanding of this struggle by exploring the archetypes and collective unconscious that shape human experience across cultures and time. This depth-psychological perspective complements GCT's recognition that the journey from ego-centered to heart-centered awareness is not merely personal but connects to universal patterns of human development. Both approaches invite us to view individual healing as part of a larger evolutionary process that transcends the merely personal while honoring each person's unique journey.

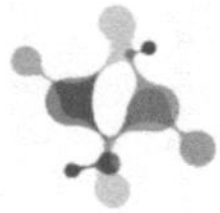
Jungian

## 6.7 Jungian Approaches and GCT

Jungian psychology emphasizes archetypes, the collective unconscious, and the lifelong process of individuation—the journey toward integrating the many aspects of the self (Jung, 1968). In my experience, these concepts align closely with GCT's core emphasis on re-centering the heart and activating the observer. Through techniques such as dream analysis and active imagination, I have observed that clients can access universal symbolic patterns that illuminate their inner conflicts and healing potential. GCT enhances this work by providing concrete methods—such as observer activation and heart-centered reframing—to ground these symbolic insights into measurable and practical steps. This integration allows clients not only to explore the depths of their unconscious but also to translate these insights into intentional, real-world change.

*Reflective Prompt:*
How might exploring archetypal symbols and the collective unconscious with your clients deepen their process of individuation and alignment?

While Jungian approaches offer profound insights into the depths of the collective unconscious, their abstract nature can sometimes be challenging to translate into concrete therapeutic interventions. Transactional Analysis (TA) provides a complementary framework with its clear, accessible model of Parent, Adult, and

Child ego states. This structural understanding of personality dovetails with GCT's delineation of the various egoic lenses, offering practical language for identifying patterns of interaction both internally and interpersonally. Both TA and GCT recognize that transformation requires awareness of these patterns and intentional shifts in how we engage with ourselves and others.

### 6.8 Transactional Analysis and GCT

Transactional Analysis (TA) offers a straightforward yet powerful framework for understanding the dynamics between the Parent, Adult, and Child ego states (Berne, 1964). In my practice, TA's delineation of these states provides clarity in deciphering how clients interact with themselves and others. GCT builds on this by mapping these ego states onto its own framework—particularly by identifying which of the egoic lenses (such as the critic or bully) dominate a client's internal dialogue. When a client becomes aware that their Parent (often critical) or Child (often vulnerable) state is in control, GCT interventions help shift them toward the Adult state—mirrored by the observer's balanced perspective and the heart's compassionate guidance. This combined approach supports clients in rewriting their internal scripts and cultivating more balanced, authentic transactions in their relationships.

*Reflective Prompt:*
How might incorporating the TA model alongside GCT tools help clients identify and reframe unproductive internal scripts in their everyday interactions?

Transactional Analysis illuminates the structure and dynamics of internal and external transactions, yet it may not fully address the broader question of purpose and contribution that many clients seek. Adlerian psychology enriches our understanding by emphasizing social interest and the human drive for significance as core motivational forces. This focus on meaningful contribution aligns with GCT's emphasis on intentional evolution and the heart's natural orientation toward reciprocal connection. Both approaches recognize that healing is not complete until it extends beyond individual well-being to encompass one's relationship with the larger community and one's authentic contribution to life.

AA

### 6.9 Adlerian Approaches and GCT

Adlerian psychology, with its focus on social interest, inferiority, and the striving for significance, provides profound insights into how early experiences shape our drive for personal growth and community contribution (Adler, 1956). I have found that Adler's emphasis on the individual's role in society dovetails neatly with GCT's call for intentional evolution. Whereas Adler highlights the compensatory mechanisms that arise from feelings of inferiority, GCT encourages a re-centering of the heart that transforms these mechanisms into a source of authentic self-worth and social interest. In practice, integrating Adlerian techniques—such as exploring early recollections and establishing purposeful goals—with GCT's methods helps clients move from a state of ego-driven compensation to one of genuine, heart-led connection with themselves and their communities.

*Reflective Prompt:*
In what ways can exploring early recollections and feelings of inferiority, through an Adlerian lens, support a client's journey toward authentic self-acceptance and social interest when combined with GCT?

While Adlerian psychology emphasizes purpose and contribution in a social context, Gestalt therapy brings our attention back to the immediate, lived experience of the present moment. This here-and-now focus complements GCT's emphasis on observer activation and present-centered awareness as foundations for transformation. Both approaches recognize that genuine change occurs not through intellectual understanding alone but through direct, embodied experience of one's reality. The Gestalt principle of awareness leading to natural change parallels GCT's understanding that when the observer is activated and the heart centered, the psyche naturally moves toward greater alignment and integration.

GESTALT

### 6.10 Gestalt Theory and GCT

Gestalt therapy emphasizes the importance of present-moment awareness and taking responsibility for one's experiences (Perls, Hefferline, & Goodman, 1951). In my work, I have seen that the Gestalt focus on "here-and-now" experience dovetails perfectly with GCT's emphasis on observer activation and heart-centered alignment. By using Gestalt techniques such as the empty chair or role-playing exercises, clients learn to become fully aware of their immediate sensations and emotions. GCT enhances these practices by offering structured methods to separate raw feelings from re-enacted past narratives—allowing clients to process their experiences authentically. This approach fosters an integrated self that takes responsibility for its own healing, transforming present-moment awareness into a powerful catalyst for change.

*Reflective Prompt:*
How might you use Gestalt exercises, combined with GCT's observer and heart practices, to help clients experience the present moment more fully and authentically?'

Gestalt therapy's emphasis on present-moment awareness and experiential engagement provides powerful tools for immediate transformation, yet many clients also seek meaning and connection

n that transcend individual experience. Transpersonal approaches address this dimension directly by exploring states of consciousness and connection that extend beyond the personal self. This expansive perspective complements GCT's recognition that heart-centered awareness naturally opens to a sense of universal connection and meaning. Both approaches acknowledge that healing at its deepest level involves not just resolving personal issues but also awakening to a larger sense of being and purpose that transcends ego-based identity.

## 6.11 Transpersonal Approaches and GCT

Transpersonal psychology explores the spiritual dimensions of human experience, emphasizing that true healing involves transcending the ego to access higher states of consciousness (Walsh & Vaughan, 1993). In my experience, transpersonal approaches enrich GCT by addressing the "what" and "why" questions that many other models neglect. By integrating practices such as meditation, guided visualizations, and reflective inquiry into the nature of existence, I help clients connect with a sense of meaning and purpose that goes beyond everyday concerns. GCT's framework—which prioritizes intentional evolution and re-centering the heart—provides a solid, structured basis for these transpersonal explorations. This integration encourages clients to see their personal struggles as part of a larger, interconnected whole, fostering a sense of universal connection that transcends cultural, racial, and gender differences.

*Reflective Prompt:*
How can integrating transpersonal practices into your sessions help

clients answer the deeper "what" and "why" of their existence? What spiritual exercises have you found particularly effective in promoting a sense of universal connection?

**Conclusion of Chapter Six**

This chapter has demonstrated how Gifted Compassionate Therapy integrates various psychotherapeutic models—from CBT to transpersonal approaches—into a cohesive, holistic framework. Each model contributes unique insights that, when combined with the GCT principles of the observer, heart, ego, and spirit, form a powerful roadmap for intentional evolution and healing. Together, these integrated approaches empower clinicians to transcend traditional symptom management and guide clients toward deeper self-awareness, genuine connection, and systemic transformation.

As you continue your journey with GCT, consider how these diverse modalities can be adapted and integrated into your own practice. The tools and insights offered here provide a robust foundation for a transformative, heart-centered approach to therapy—one that honors the full spectrum of human experience and fosters a more humane, connected world.

- **Integration of Models:**
  GCT serves as a unifying framework that highlights the interdependence of the observer, spirit, ego, and heart. It expands on the strengths of established modalities while addressing their limitations—particularly in terms of accessing deeper emotional and intuitive wisdom.

- **Practical Applications:**
  Each integration—from thought records with observer activation in CBT to heart-centered reparenting in IFS, and from body scans in somatic therapy to exploring

transference in psychodynamic work—illustrates actionable steps toward alignment.

- **Clinical Synergy:**
  The synergy between GCT and these traditional models is evident in the way therapeutic interventions are enhanced. For example, GCT's emphasis on the heart's compassion enriches DBT's mindfulness practices, while its identification of egoic lenses deepens the insights gained from IFS.

- **Addressing Ego Dysfunction:**
  For clients with narcissistic traits and other manifestations of ego dysfunction, GCT provides a pathway that bypasses resistance and re-centers the heart, offering hope for both personal healing and the alleviation of relational harm.

- **Broad Applicability:**
  The integrative approach of GCT not only supports individual transformation but also has broader systemic implications—promoting healthier relationships, community well-being, and even organizational change.

**Reflective Prompt:**
As you reflect on the integration of these psychotherapeutic models with GCT, consider which aspects resonate most with your practice. How might you synthesize these diverse approaches into a coherent treatment plan that aligns with the principles of intentional evolution?

### Future Directions and Systemic Implications

The work of integrating diverse psychotherapeutic models is ongoing. Future research in neuroplasticity, heart coherence, and trauma-informed care will undoubtedly refine these approaches further. Moreover, the systemic implications of GCT's integrative model—its potential to inspire change at community and organizational levels—are ripe areas for exploration. As practitioners, continuing to adapt and refine these interventions will be essential in meeting the complex needs of our clients.

**Final Transitional Note**

As we've explored these diverse therapeutic approaches, a consistent pattern emerges: each modality offers valuable insights and techniques that address specific dimensions of human experience, yet each also has natural limitations. GCT does not replace these approaches but rather provides an integrative framework that honors their contributions while addressing their limitations. The unifying principles across all these modalities—observer awareness, heart-centered compassion, recognition of protective ego functions, and the potential for intentional evolution—form the foundation of GCT's holistic approach. By weaving together these complementary perspectives, therapists can create a more comprehensive and effective approach to healing that honors the full complexity of human experience while providing clear pathways for transformation.

# Chapter Eight
# GCT in Action—Real-Life Cases

**Introduction: Setting the Stage for GCT in Action**

Gifted Compassionate Therapy (GCT) is a comprehensive, integrative framework for healing that combines assessment, alignment, and heart-centered interventions to address a broad spectrum of psychological, emotional, and relational challenges. Whereas previous chapters have outlined the underlying principles and integration of GCT with established psychotherapeutic models, this chapter focuses on the application of GCT to real-life cases. Each case illustrates how GCT's unique approach transforms the therapeutic process, guiding clients toward deeper alignment, intentional evolution, and a marked reduction in suffering.

Central to the effectiveness of GCT is its emphasis on holistic assessment before treatment. The comprehensive intake process is designed not only to capture a client's symptomatic presentation but also to explore the internal landscape—from cognitive styles and emotional patterns to instinctual responses and placement on the humane spectrum. This in-depth assessment ensures that interventions are precisely tailored to address the root causes of disconnection and misalignment, while simultaneously offering a roadmap for growth and transformation.

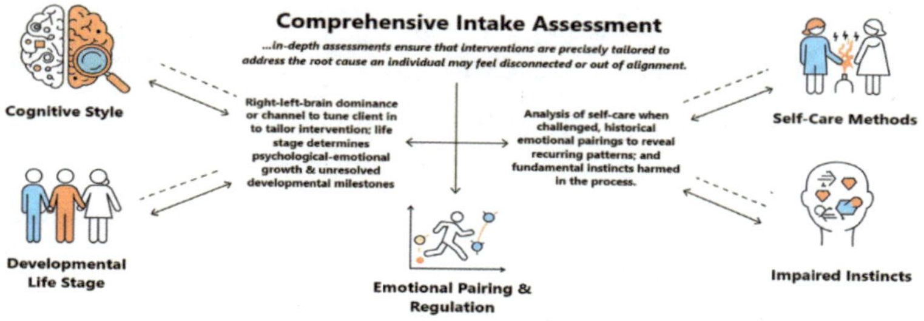


## GCT's Comprehensive Intake Assessment

In GCT, the intake phase is far more than a diagnostic exercise—it is an opportunity to engage the client in a reflective, humane exploration of their inner world. This phase integrates projective and functional measures to capture the nuances of a client's cognitive style, emotional patterns, and instinctual tendencies, as well as their current alignment on the humane spectrum. In doing so, it lays the groundwork for personalized interventions that honor the client's unique experience and foster intentional evolution.

Key elements include:

- **Projective and Functional Measures:**
  • *Cognitive Style:* Assessment of right- or left-brain dominance and preferred learning modalities, thereby tailoring interventions to a client's natural strengths (Vecchio, 2025).
  • *Developmental Life Stage:* Evaluation of the client's psychological and emotional growth, identifying unresolved developmental milestones that may shape current behavior.
  • *Self-Care Preference:* Analysis of instinctual approaches to self-care—whether clients tend to fight, avoid, submit, compromise, or collaborate when challenged.

• *Affective Pairings:* Mapping of dominant emotional pairings (e.g., sadness with guilt or anger with frustration) to reveal recurring patterns that contribute to suffering.
• *Instinctual Impairments:* Examination of how past experiences have impacted fundamental instincts such as trust, intimacy, and safety.
• *Emotional Thermometer:* Measurement of emotional regulation and reactivity, indicating a client's capacity to process and respond to emotional stimuli.

- **Placement on the Humane Spectrum:**
  This diagnostic tool maps a client's current state of alignment along a continuum ranging from egocentricity to compassionate reciprocity (Vecchio, 2025). It highlights which egoic lens—critic, bully, mediator, or counselor—is most dominant and pinpoints areas ripe for transformation.

**Mapping the Mind, Heart, and Gut for Holistic Alignment**

In this chapter, GCT would be amiss if it didn't expand on the client's cognitive style and how using such information distinguishes this therapy from more conventional approaches. A key component of GCT's intake assessment is analyzing a client's existing neuropsychological test results. These scores provide a valuable glimpse into how they process information—revealing whether they are primarily "in their head" with left-brain dominance or more attuned to context and emotion via right-brain functions.

Understanding a client's cognitive style is a critical first step. When we know in advance where someone is operating on this continuum, we can tailor our interventions to help them tap into the full potential of their inner resources. In GCT, the goal is to move beyond a purely analytical, left-brain approach. We aim to encourage a more integrated, "whole-brained" state that embraces not only the mind but also the heart and gut—the centers of emotional insight and instinctual wisdom.

Importantly, this initial mapping is our first glimpse at where the client might land on the Humane Spectrum. Although we have not yet fully explored their presenting problems, these scores are a critical indicator. They help us recognize if they rely heavily on rational analysis at the expense of emotional and somatic awareness. By identifying this imbalance early on, we can design interventions that specifically encourage the client to engage their heart (for compassion and intuitive insight) and their gut (for instinctual, embodied understanding).

Ultimately, this knowledge is not an endpoint but a starting point. It enables us to customize treatment, guiding clients toward a more balanced, integrative approach. When the mind relaxes its overcontrol, the heart and gut can step in—supporting a more holistic, self-correcting system that fosters genuine healing and intentional evolution.

This is the power of knowing where a client is "in their head" from the very beginning—it sets the stage for unlocking the full spectrum of human experience and transformation.

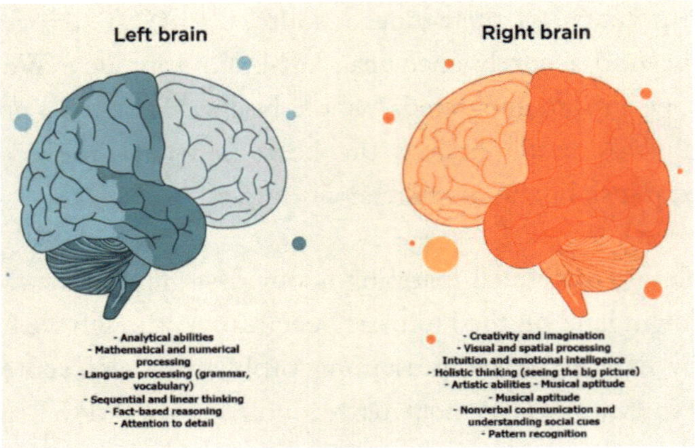


## Neuropsychological Test Scores in GCT's Comprehensive Intake: A Practical Example

| Index/Subtest | Score | Hemisphere Dominance |
|---|---|---|
| Verbal Comprehension Index (VCI) | 95 | Left |
| - Similarities | 10 | Left |
| - Vocabulary | 9 | Left |
| - Information | 8 | Left |
| Perceptual Reasoning Index (PRI) | 110 | Right |
| - Block Design | 12 | Right |
| - Matrix Reasoning | 11 | Right |
| - Visual Puzzles | 13 | Right |
| Working Memory Index (WMI) | 85 | Left |
| - Digit Span | 7 | Left |
| - Arithmetic | 8 | Left |
| Processing Speed Index (PSI) | 90 | Right |
| - Symbol Search | 9 | Right |
| - Coding | 8 | Right |
| Full Scale IQ (FSIQ) | 95 | - |

Above is an example of how GCT leverages a client's Wechsler Adult Intelligence Scale) scores to leverage interventions. We see in this example that the client's **Verbal Comprehension** (VCI) and **Working Memory** (WMI) indices lean left-brain, whereas **Perceptual Reasoning** (PRI) and **Processing Speed** (PSI) show right-brain dominance. The **Full-Scale IQ** (FSIQ) is 95, suggesting an overall average range of functioning. This "scatter" in subtest scores is not just academic data—it reveals how the client naturally takes in, processes, and expresses information.

**Why This Matters for GCT**

**a. Identifies Cognitive Style and Hemisphere Dominance**

GCT holds that understanding whether a client is more left-brain, or right-brain dominant helps tailor interventions to their natural strengths:

- **Left-Brain Dominance:** Typically suggests a client who processes material verbally, analytically, and in a linear fashion. Such individuals may excel at rational problem-solving but can struggle to integrate emotional or contextual nuances.
- **Right-Brain Dominance:** Often indicates strengths in spatial reasoning, pattern recognition, and emotional/ contextual processing. These clients may be more intuitive and creative but might have difficulty articulating detailed, sequential information.

For the example above, the client shows a modest advantage in right-brain tasks (higher PRI and some aspects of WMI, plus strong coding and symbol search), yet their verbal comprehension and part of working memory are left-brain oriented. This combination suggests they can handle analytical tasks but also have a capacity for visual-spatial and intuitive problem-solving.

**b. Linking Cognitive Style to GCT's Goals**

In GCT, we aim to foster **whole-brained** functioning. While left-brain dominance can keep a client "in their head," right-brain dominance may enhance emotional or contextual insight. We want to ensure neither hemisphere overpowers the other. By relaxing the grip of an overactive left brain, for instance, a client gains greater access to the heart (emotional intelligence) and "stomach" (instinctual awareness), enabling intentional evolution.

**Practical Example: Using This Data in a Session**

**Step 1: Explaining the Findings**

During the intake, the therapist might say:

"Your scores show that you're fairly comfortable with words and logic (Verbal Comprehension), but you also have strengths in visual reasoning (Perceptual Reasoning). This suggests you can approach problems both analytically and intuitively, though you might lean more on one style than the other in stressful situations."

**Step 2: Tailoring Interventions**

1. **Observer Activation (Left-Right Integration):**
    - **Approach:** Start each session with a guided mindfulness exercise.
    - **Rationale:** A client with a decent right-brain capacity for context might find it easier to visualize tension or notice bodily sensations. Yet, they may also revert to left-brain analysis under stress. Prompt them to observe thoughts and emotions

without dissecting them immediately, balancing both hemispheres.

2. **Heart-Centered Reframing (Engaging Right Brain Intuition):**
    - **Approach:** Use guided imagery to help the client visualize their heart as a central, warm compass.
    - **Rationale:** Because they have strong visual-spatial skills (PRI of 110), imaginative exercises that tap into metaphor and imagery will likely resonate. Encourage them to pair these images with verbal self-affirmations, thereby integrating left-brain language skills.
3. **Verbal-Analytical Check-Ins (Left-Brain Comfort Zone):**
    - **Approach:** Have the client keep a daily thought log, focusing on identifying specific triggers and the negative beliefs tied to them.
    - **Rationale:** Their comfort with verbal tasks (VCI of 95) can help them articulate internal dialogues. Then, gently shift to heart-based language to reframe those beliefs.
4. **Processing Speed and Grounding Techniques:**
    - **Approach:** Because their Processing Speed Index (PSI) is 90, they might benefit from structured, timed grounding exercises that do not overwhelm them with rapid instructions.

- **Rationale:** Provide enough time for the client to integrate each step, balancing both quick emotional check-ins and structured, methodical steps.

### Step 3: Integrating the Findings for Intentional Evolution

After introducing these interventions, the therapist continually references the test scores to remind the client how they process information. For example:

"Remember, you have a natural ability to see patterns quickly (right-brain strength). Let's use that skill to identify when your critic lens is popping up in your daily thoughts. We can then reframe it with a heart-centered approach."

Over time, the client learns to harness their left-brain analytical skills without becoming stuck in overthinking, while also leveraging their right-brain capacity for emotional and contextual insight. This synergy fosters whole-brained integration, aligning with GCT's ultimate goal: re-centering the heart, reducing ego distortions, and engaging in intentional evolution.

### 4. Why Therapists Should Use Previous Testing in Intake

- **Customized Interventions:** By understanding the client's cognitive style, therapists can adapt session strategies (e.g., journaling vs. guided imagery) to match how the client naturally learns.
- **Reduced Frustration:** Clients often feel more at ease when the therapy aligns with their processing strengths. Conversely, if we force a left-brain approach on a client who thrives on visual or emotional insight, progress can stall.

- **Deeper Engagement:** Emphasizing the client's strengths (e.g., right-brain creativity) can boost self-esteem and motivation. A client who sees how their natural capacities can aid in healing is more likely to commit to the therapeutic process.
- **Intentional Evolution:** GCT frames these neuropsychological insights not as static labels, but as guides for how to unify analytical, emotional, and instinctual intelligence, thereby promoting holistic growth.

### Beyond Diagnosis: GCT's Unique Perspective

Traditional diagnostic frameworks tend to label and categorize conditions such as PTSD, anxiety, or depression. GCT, however, views these diagnoses as markers of misalignment rather than as permanent states. For example, PTSD is understood as the psyche's attempt to integrate overwhelming experiences, often resulting in hypervigilance or avoidance. In GCT, this is reframed as an urgent call to reconnect with safety and the heart's guidance. Similarly, anxiety may reflect the overactivity of the critic lens, while depression may signal the gravitational pull of spiritual disconnection. By shifting the focus from pathology to possibility, GCT reveals each condition as an opportunity for intentional growth.

*Reflective Prompt:*
Consider a client whose self-reported diagnosis seems to mask deeper internal dynamics. How might you use GCT's intake process to reveal and address these underlying misalignments?

### GCT in Action: A Framework for Case Examples

The following real-life cases demonstrate how GCT is applied in diverse clinical contexts. Each case includes:

1. **Assessment Phase:**
   Use of GCT's intake tools to map cognitive style, emotional patterns, instinctual impairments, and humane spectrum placement.

2. **Core Misalignment:**
   Exploration of the root causes of suffering—whether through egoic distortions, misaligned instincts, or unresolved emotional wounds.

3. **Intervention and Realignment:**
   Application of GCT techniques (observer activation, heart-centered reflection, and ego reframing) to guide the client toward deeper alignment.

4. **Outcome and Reflection:**
   Evaluation of progress in emotional regulation, relational functioning, and overall reduction in suffering.

**Case #1: Reframing the Inner Critic—A Journey to Self-Compassion**

When Case #1, a 31-year-old male, entered therapy, he reported a life dominated by internal chaos and external instability. Although his substance use was in remission, he described being haunted by relentless inner criticism and chronic self-blame. His relationships were unstable, marked by a fear of vulnerability and impulsive withdrawal when confronted with emotional intimacy.

A thorough GCT intake revealed that his placement on the humane spectrum was skewed toward egocentricity, with the critic and bully lenses dominating his inner dialogue. His emotional thermometer indicated low distress tolerance, with sadness and guilt frequently escalating into reactive behaviors. Additionally, personality traits such as histrionic sensitivity and antisocial impulsivity compounded his struggles, while avoidant and dependent tendencies created a push-pull dynamic that further isolated him.

At the core of his suffering was a profound lack of self-compassion. Disconnected from his heart lens, he had come to rely on external validation and ego-driven coping mechanisms to navigate his pain. He felt like a passive observer in his own life, unable to steer his emotional course.

**The Healing Process:**

- **Activating the Observer:**
  The journey began by cultivating his observer—a neutral, nonjudgmental presence that allowed him to step back from reactive patterns. Although confronting the inner critic and bully lenses was initially unsettling, this process revealed that these parts were not inherent flaws, but rather protective responses formed in response to early rejection.

- **Engaging with Internal Family Systems (IFS):**
  Through IFS work, the client engaged directly with these parts. The critic, originating from conditional approval in childhood, and the bully, serving as a shield against vulnerability, were both acknowledged and given space. The heart lens offered a compassionate reframe: "You've been trying to protect me, but I don't need to be perfect to be worthy."

- **Integrating CBT and DBT Techniques:**
  CBT tools helped him challenge distorted thoughts, such as "I'm a failure," while DBT skills like mindfulness and radical acceptance provided strategies for managing overwhelming emotions without avoidance. Grounding

exercises helped him to remain present, reducing the tendency to react impulsively.

- **Somatic Interventions:**
  Somatic therapy revealed that chronic chest tension was a physical manifestation of suppressed sadness. Guided body scans and mindful movement allowed him to release this tension, reconnecting him with his body as a source of strength.

By the end of therapy, Case #1 experienced a profound transformation. The dominance of the critic and bully lenses was softened, and the heart lens began to guide his self-perception with compassion and authenticity. Emotional regulation improved markedly, and his relationships evolved from cycles of isolation and impulsivity to spaces of genuine connection. His journey demonstrated that healing was not about eliminating pain but about transforming it into a resource for growth.

*Reflective Prompt:*
How has witnessing a client's inner critic as a protective mechanism influenced your approach to fostering self-compassion in therapy?

**Clinical Application Points: Transforming the Inner Critic**

**Key Assessment Insights:**

- Dominant critic and bully lenses can mask underlying vulnerability and need for self-compassion
- Note how substance use may function as temporary relief from self-criticism
- Identify emotional pairings (in this case, sadness-guilt) that trigger reactive patterns

**Effective Interventions:**

- **Observer Activation Technique:** Start sessions with 2-3 minutes of mindful awareness, asking "What is noticing these thoughts right now?"
- **IFS-Informed Dialogue:** Use phrases like "Let's speak directly to this critical part" to externalize and engage with the critic lens
- **Heart-Centered Reframing:** Guide clients to place a hand on their heart while offering self-compassion statements: "I'm doing the best I can with what I know right now"

**Implementation Timeline:**

- First 3-4 sessions: Focus on observer activation and emotional safety
- Middle phase (sessions 5-12): Engage directly with critic and bully lenses
- Later sessions: Cultivate self-compassion and heart-centered perspective

**Challenges to Anticipate:**

- Initial resistance to self-compassion (skepticism, unworthiness)
- Grief that may emerge as critical protection mechanisms are released
- "Backlash effect" when the inner critic temporarily intensifies

## Case #2: Navigating Transitions—From Emotional Avoidance to Authentic Presence

### Presenting Problem and Diagnostic Context

Case #2 is a 20-year-old female presenting with a complex history of anxiety, depression, and emotional detachment, compounded by obsessive-compulsive behaviors. Although her symptoms have partially improved with medication, she continues to struggle with emotional regulation, crying spells, and episodes of numbness. In addition, she faces challenges with focus and long-term goal setting. Her intake assessment placed her toward the egocentric end of the humane spectrum, dominated by the critic and mediator lenses. These lenses amplify self-doubt and drive her tendency to sacrifice her own needs to maintain external harmony.

Developmentally, she is at a critical juncture where identity formation and independence are paramount. However, unresolved early attachments and a pervasive need for external validation hinder her progress.

### The Healing Journey:

- **Observer Activation:**
  Early sessions focused on cultivating her observer. Through mindfulness and reflective practices, she began to discern how her mediator lens—aimed at preserving harmony—clashed with her deeper emotional needs.

- **Exploring Attachment Patterns:**
  Psychodynamic exploration revealed that her mediator lens developed as a response to early experiences where maintaining harmony was essential for emotional safety. By re-engaging with her heart lens, she learned to view

these patterns as protective but outdated, enabling her to honor her own needs.

- **Integrating CBT and DBT:**
  CBT techniques were employed to challenge catastrophic thoughts linked to her perfectionistic tendencies. DBT skills, such as grounding exercises and radical acceptance, helped her navigate overwhelming emotional states.

- **Somatic Awareness:**
  Somatic therapy uncovered physical tension in her shoulders and jaw, which corresponded to unresolved grief. Through body scans and mindful movement, she began to release this tension, reconnecting with her body.

- **Humanistic and Existential Exploration:**
  Reflecting on her values and aspirations allowed her to reconnect with a sense of purpose. She began to take small, meaningful steps—journaling, volunteering, and fostering reciprocal relationships.

- **Spiritual Practices:**
  Transpersonal practices, including guided meditations, deepened her awareness of interconnectedness and instilled hope that her struggles were part of a larger journey of growth.

Over time, Case #2 demonstrated significant progress. Her ability to regulate emotions improved, and the dominance of the critic and mediator lenses diminished. She set healthier boundaries and experienced relationships that were more balanced and supportive. Her vocational engagement and creative pursuits gradually flourished as she embraced a mindset of progress rather than perfection.

*Reflective Prompt:*
How can integrating somatic and transpersonal practices enrich the treatment of clients struggling with emotional avoidance?

**Clinical Application Points: Addressing Emotional Avoidance**

**Key Assessment Insights:**

- Mediator lens often indicates early adaptive patterns where emotional authenticity was unsafe
- Developmental stage (identity formation) requires particular attention to autonomy and authentic expression
- Emotional numbing serves a protective function that must be honored before change can occur

**Effective Interventions:**

- **Emotional Validation Sequence:** "Your avoidance makes perfect sense, given your experiences" → "This protection served you well" → "There are new possibilities available now"
- **Somatic Bridging Technique:** Guide attention to physical sensations associated with emotions before attempting to name the emotions
- **Progressive Exposure to Feelings:** Use 0-10 scale to titrate emotional engagement, respecting the client's window of tolerance

**Implementation Timeline:**

- Early sessions: Focus on safety, containment, and observer activation

- Middle phase: Gradually introduce small "doses" of emotional engagement
- Later sessions: Practice authentic emotional expression in safe relationships

**Documentation Considerations:**

- Track specific body sensations associated with emotional avoidance
- Note shifts in emotional vocabulary and expression over time
- Document increasing capacity for dual awareness (feeling emotions while maintaining observer perspective)

## Case #3: From Emotional Avoidance to Empowered Connection

### Presenting Problem and Diagnostic Context

Case #3 is a 35-year-old female whose lifelong struggle with depression, anxiety, emotional avoidance, and self-harm has deeply affected her personal and professional life. With a history of multiple diagnoses—including Persistent Depressive Disorder, Generalized Anxiety Disorder, and early ADHD—she reports pervasive self-doubt, perfectionism, and difficulty accessing joy. Despite some symptom relief through medication, she continues to experience emotional detachment and self-blame.

Her intake assessment revealed that her placement on the humane spectrum was heavily skewed by the critic and mediator lenses. These lenses drive her perfectionism and cause her to prioritize harmony at the expense of her authentic self-expression, resulting in chronic emotional avoidance.

**The Healing Journey:**

- **Observer Activation and Awareness:**
  Therapy began by cultivating her observer, enabling her to detach from the automatic self-judgment generated by her critic lens. Early breakthroughs emerged when she could identify and label her emotions without being overwhelmed by them.

- **Psychodynamic Exploration:**
  Delving into the origins of her internal critic and mediator lenses uncovered the impact of early experiences of rejection and conditional acceptance. The heart lens was introduced as a compassionate guide to reframe these patterns.

- **Cognitive-Behavioral and DBT Interventions:**
  Using CBT, she learned to reframe self-critical thoughts (e.g., "If I don't succeed perfectly, I'm a failure") into more balanced statements. DBT grounding exercises further helped her manage overwhelming emotions in real time.

- **Gestalt and Existential Approaches:**
  Reflecting on her values and aspirations, she began to reconnect with her creative passions and set small, achievable goals. This shift from striving for perfection to embracing progress marked a turning point in her recovery.

- **Somatic and Psychospiritual Integration:**
  Somatic therapy revealed that her chronic tension in the jaw and chest corresponded with her unresolved grief. Through mindful movement and visualizations focusing

on the heart lens, she experienced moments of relief and a renewed sense of connection.

- **Transformation and Relational Growth:**
  As therapy progressed, her internal critic softened, and the heart's guidance became more pronounced. She developed healthier boundaries in relationships and began to engage in reciprocal, authentic connections. Vocationally, she explored new avenues aligned with her values, gradually redefining success on her own terms.

*Reflective Prompt:*
How do you help clients move from a state of emotional avoidance to one of empowered connection? Which interventions have you found most transformative in fostering self-compassion and authenticity?

**Clinical Application Points: Depression, Anxiety, and Self-Harm**

**Key Assessment Insights:**

- Critic and mediator lenses often co-occur in perfectionistic clients with depression
- Self-harm may function as emotional regulation when authentic expression feels unsafe
- Assessment should identify specific triggers for emotional detachment

**Effective Interventions:**

- **Cognitive-Somatic Integration:** Pair cognitive reframing with specific body-based grounding techniques

- **Heart-Lens Dialogue Template:** "If your heart could speak to this situation, what might it say that your critic cannot?"
- **Titrated Exposure to Authenticity:** Create hierarchies of emotional vulnerability, starting with safer contexts

**Risk Management Considerations:**

- Establish clear safety protocols for self-harm urges
- Develop "emotional emergency kit" with specific self-soothing techniques
- Create gradual timeline for reducing avoidance behaviors to prevent overwhelming activation

**Measurement of Progress:**

- Reduction in emotional avoidance behaviors (quantify frequency)
- Increased emotional vocabulary and differentiation
- Improved interpersonal boundaries and authentic self-expression

## Case #4: From Emotional Detachment to Empowered Connection

### Presenting Problem and Diagnostic Context

Case #4 is a 26-year-old female with Persistent Depressive Disorder, Adjustment Disorder with Mixed Features, ADHD Inattentive Type, and a Specific Learning Disorder. Her struggles are compounded by obesity and Duane Retraction Syndrome, which have contributed to lifelong feelings of being "othered." She reports significant anxiety triggered by disruptions to routine, leading to irritability, emotional detachment, and pervasive self-doubt. Early experiences of hazing and mistreatment have entrenched her critic and mediator lenses, which fuel self-criticism and conformity at the expense of emotional authenticity.

**The Healing Journey:**

- **Observer Activation:**
  The therapy process began by cultivating her observer, allowing her to step back from her automatic defensive patterns. This practice enabled her to discern how her critic lens amplified her feelings of inadequacy.

- **Psychodynamic and Attachment Work:**
  Exploring her early experiences revealed that her self-critical beliefs were deeply rooted in past mistreatment. The heart lens was introduced as a means to reframe these early wounds with compassion: "You deserve love and connection just as you are."

- **Integration of CBT and Somatic Techniques:**
  Through CBT, she learned to challenge distortions like "My worth depends on others' approval." Concurrently, somatic interventions helped her release chronic tension in her chest and abdomen—physical manifestations of suppressed grief and self-doubt.

- **Boundary-Setting and Humanistic Approaches:**
  Gradually, she learned to assert her needs in relationships, transitioning from a pattern of over-conformity to one of reciprocal connection.

- **Psychospiritual Integration:**
  Guided meditations and visualizations reinforced her

sense of belonging and authenticity, helping her view her differences as strengths rather than deficits.

By the end of therapy, Case #4 experienced a significant transformation. Her internal dialogue shifted from self-criticism to self-compassion. She began setting healthy boundaries, fostering relationships that honored her authentic needs, and pursuing vocational opportunities that aligned with her values.

*Reflective Prompt:*
In what ways have you seen boundary-setting improve a client's relational dynamics? How might you support clients in integrating somatic and psychospiritual practices to overcome self-criticism?

**Clinical Application Points: Addressing "Othering" and Self-Worth**

**Key Assessment Insights:**

- Physical differences and past mistreatment often create complex layers of shame
- Critic and mediator lenses may function as protection against further rejection
- Assessment should explore specific contexts where authenticity feels most/least safe

**Effective Interventions:**

- **Protective Parts Dialogue:** "Let's thank this protective part for trying to keep you safe, even as we explore new possibilities"
- **Boundary Rehearsal Protocol:** Use role-play to practice setting boundaries with graduated levels of difficulty

- **Somatic Resourcing:** Establish physical anchors for safety before processing difficult emotions

**Adapting for Physical Differences:**

- Modify somatic interventions to accommodate physical limitations
- Use client's unique physical experience as source of wisdom and perspective
- Reframe physical differences as potential sources of insight and connection

**Cultural Considerations:**

- Address internalized prejudice from societal messaging about "normalcy"
- Explore how cultural expectations impact self-perception
- Incorporate relevant cultural strengths and resources into treatment plan

## Case #5: From Dependence to Empowered Autonomy

### Presenting Problem and Diagnostic Context

Case #5 is a 38-year-old male with Persistent Depressive Disorder, a history of Substance Use Disorder (in remission), and features of Personality Disorder NOS, including borderline, avoidant, dependent, and negativistic traits. He also grapples with a Learning Disorder NOS and significant physical challenges due to spinal stenosis. Although he has maintained sobriety for over 11 months and reports improvements in anxiety, he continues to struggle with depression, self-doubt, and a diminished sense of autonomy.

His intake assessment revealed misalignments rooted in unresolved grief, physical pain, and personality patterns characterized by a dominant critic lens and a reactive bully lens. These factors, compounded by his reliance on external validation, have hindered his journey toward self-reliance and independence.

**The Healing Journey:**

- **Activating the Observer:**
  Therapy began by helping him cultivate his observer, allowing him to recognize the patterns of self-criticism and defensiveness that had long undermined his self-worth. One breakthrough came when he realized, "I've been fighting myself as much as I've been fighting others."

- **Psychodynamic Exploration and Family History:**
  Exploration of his early family dynamics—marked by instability and substance misuse—revealed how these experiences shaped his dependency patterns. The heart lens was introduced as a source of internal validation: "You are enough as you are." This shift allowed him to start dismantling the defenses of his critic and bully lenses.

- **CBT and DBT Interventions:**
  CBT techniques helped him reframe thoughts such as "I'll never be able to accomplish anything with this pain." DBT skills, including distress tolerance and mindfulness, provided him with practical tools to manage emotional surges. Grounding exercises and radical acceptance practices became integral to his daily routine.

- **Somatic and Existential Work:**
  Somatic therapy revealed chronic tension in his lower back and shoulders, which he learned to release through

mindful movement. Concurrently, existential explorations helped him redefine independence as the ability to make empowered choices despite limitations.

- **Psychospiritual Integration:**
  Guided meditations and visualizations allowed him to envision his recovery as part of a larger journey. Over time, he began to see his physical limitations not as defining weaknesses, but as challenges to be managed with resilience and purpose.

By the conclusion of therapy, Case #5 experienced a profound shift—from dependence and self-doubt to empowered autonomy. His internal critic and bully softened as he learned to trust his heart, setting healthy boundaries with family members and embracing a flexible, purpose-driven approach to his career and personal life.

*Reflective Prompt:*
How do you help clients reframe physical limitations and unresolved grief as opportunities for growth? What strategies have been most effective in fostering empowered autonomy?

**Clinical Application Points: Chronic Pain and Recovery**

**Key Assessment Insights:**

- Physical pain often exacerbates dependency patterns and heightens ego defensiveness
- Addiction history may complicate emotional regulation and self-trust
- Multiple personality traits require flexible, integrated intervention approach

**Effective Interventions:**

- **Pain-Emotion Differentiation Technique:** Guide clients to distinguish between physical pain and emotional suffering
- **Incremental Autonomy Protocol:** Create hierarchy of independence-building activities calibrated to physical limitations
- **Values Clarification Timeline:** Link daily choices to broader heart-aligned values despite pain limitations

**Special Considerations for Physical Challenges:**

- Coordinate with medical providers to ensure integrated care approach
- Distinguish between physical limitations and unnecessary psychological restrictions
- Create realistic expectations that honor physical reality while promoting psychological growth

**Progress Indicators:**

- Reduced projection of blame while acknowledging legitimate limitations
- Increased self-efficacy in managing both pain and emotional responses
- Development of sustainable autonomy practices appropriate to physical condition

## Case #6: Reclaiming Vision Through Heart-Centered Reconnection

### Presenting Problem and Diagnostic Context

Case #6 a middle-aged woman experienced a cascade of trauma after being trapped in a mine collapse that fractured her back. Shortly thereafter, during a marijuana transaction, she was violently raped and brutally beaten—an assault so severe that her optic nerve was critically damaged, resulting in complete blindness within five days. Two days after the assault, she retaliated by shooting one of her attackers. Because this act was not in self-defense, she was later convicted of premeditated murder and sentenced to five years in prison. Upon incarceration, she exhibited intense hypervigilance, recurring nightmares, and profound isolation, all fueled by overwhelming anger and shame.

Assessment and Internal Mapping:

A comprehensive GCT intake revealed that her inner landscape was dominated by egoic distortions—especially the critic and bully lenses—which amplified self-blame and hyperarousal. In addition, psychodynamic assessment uncovered deep-seated early attachment wounds and unconscious conflicts related to abandonment and rejection. Despite her irreversible physical loss, evidence suggested that her innate capacity for inner vision and resilience still lay dormant beneath layers of trauma and spiritual gravity.

Treatment Process:

Establishing Safety & Observer Activation:

The initial sessions focused on building a secure, trusting therapeutic relationship. Mindfulness and grounding exercises were introduced to help her activate her internal Observer—a neutral, nonjudgmental witness to her thoughts, feelings, and bodily sensations—thus creating space between her traumatic reactions and her core self. As you might imagine it was profound to learn that though she had lost her vision—she could still see!

Heart-Centered Narrative Reframing:

The therapist guided her through narrative exercises, encouraging her to express and reframe traumatic memories. Creative imagery was used to help her visualize her heart as a steady, compassionate beacon that continues to guide her inner world even in the absence of physical sight. This intervention worked to counteract the destructive self-critical messages that had taken root over time.

Transpersonal Methods

To expand her healing beyond the personal and immediate, transpersonal practices were integrated. Guided meditations and reflective visualizations enabled her to connect with a deeper, transcendent aspect of herself—her inner "light" that had been present since birth. This work helped her frame her physical blindness not as an absolute loss, but as a doorway to spiritual awakening and broader existential meaning, fostering a sense of universal connection.

Psychodynamic Exploration:

In tandem with the above interventions, psychodynamic methods were employed to explore the unconscious roots of her distress. The therapist facilitated discussions about her early attachment experiences, uncovering unconscious patterns of abandonment and rejection that contributed to her current feelings of isolation and self-blame. Transference dynamics were gently examined, enabling her to recognize how past relational wounds were re-enacted in current interactions. This insight allowed her to begin separating the protective but ultimately maladaptive ego responses from her deeper, more authentic self.

Integration and Empowerment:

Over successive sessions, the combined effects of heart-centered, transpersonal, and psychodynamic work began to manifest. As her nightmares and flashbacks diminished, she started to reclaim a sense of internal strength and purpose. She began to articulate a redefined narrative of her life—a story where, despite the loss of physical sight, her inner vision remained potent and guiding. Ultimately, she moved from profound isolation to active engagement, volunteering in programs for blind children and sharing her journey as a testament to resilience.

Outcomes:

By the end of the treatment course, the client exhibited a marked reduction in PTSD symptoms. The regular activation of her Observer and re-centering of her heart lessened the influence of egoic distortions, while transpersonal methods provided a higher existential context that nurtured her inner light. The psychodynamic work, by bringing unconscious conflicts to awareness, enabled her to reframe deep-seated feelings of abandonment and rejection. Consequently, she transitioned from a state of isolation and overwhelming trauma to one of empowered connection—reclaiming her inner vision and a renewed sense of purpose. This case powerfully illustrates that even in the face of extreme physical and emotional loss, a comprehensive, integrative approach can lead to significant healing and intentional evolution She eventually became a blind mobility instructor to reciprocate 'give back' her experiences.

## Clinical Application Points: Severe Trauma and Blindness

### Key Assessment Insights:

- Traumatic blindness creates complex interplay between physical and psychological adaptation
- Assessment must distinguish between trauma symptoms and adaptive responses to vision loss
- Prison context creates additional safety and trust challenges

### Effective Interventions:

- **Safety-First Sequencing:** Establish consistent session structure to create predictability in unpredictable environment
- **Non-Visual Observer Activation:** Emphasize auditory, tactile, and kinesthetic cues for mindfulness practice
- **Narrative Restructuring Protocol:** Help client reorganize trauma narrative to include both loss and potential growth

### Adaptations for Vision Loss:

- Replace visual imagery with tactile, auditory, and kinesthetic metaphors
- Create multisensory grounding techniques specific to client's remaining senses
- Develop "inner vision" practices that strengthen connection to heart wisdom

### Institutional Considerations:

- Navigate prison constraints while maintaining therapeutic integrity

- Create trauma-informed coordination with prison medical/mental health staff
- Develop reintegration plan that honors both vulnerability and resilience

## Case #7: Reclaiming Strength Through Whole-Brained Integration for Teen Amputees

### Presenting Problem and Diagnostic Context

Case #7 encompasses two sixteen-year-old male adolescents experienced above-the-knee amputations—one after a fall while climbing a telephone pole and accidentally grabbing a live electric cable, and the other following a vehicular accident during an attempted escape. Although they endured nearly identical physical losses, their internal responses diverged sharply. One teen spiraled into substance abuse and suicidal ideation, while the other focused on completing his GED and planning for college. Assessment using GCT's comprehensive intake revealed that both exhibited intense trauma responses marked by dominant critic and bully lenses. However, differences in their premorbid adjustment and innate resilience provided a window for targeted intervention.

Treatment Process:

Safety and Observer Activation:

The treatment began with establishing a safe therapeutic environment. Both teens engaged in mindfulness exercises designed to cultivate their internal Observer, which helped them witness their thoughts and feelings without immediate judgment. This step laid the groundwork for recognizing ego-driven reactivity.

Heart-Centered Narrative Reframing:

In individual sessions, each teen was guided through narrative reframing exercises. The therapist used creative imagery—inviting each teen to visualize their heart as a steady, guiding beacon—to help reframe the traumatic loss from a perspective of resilience rather than victimhood. The teen on the adaptive trajectory was able to reconnect with his innate resourcefulness and envision a future beyond the trauma.

Integrated CBT and DBT Strategies:

Both adolescents received Cognitive Behavioral Therapy (CBT) interventions to challenge self-critical thoughts and Dialectical Behavior Therapy (DBT) techniques to improve emotion regulation. This dual approach helped the reactive teen reduce impulsivity and substance use while empowering the other teen to solidify his emerging academic and vocational goals.

Somatic Awareness and Expression:

Recognizing that their bodies carried the marks of trauma, somatic techniques were introduced. Guided body scans and movement-based exercises allowed each teen to sense and gradually release built-up tension. This somatic work fostered whole-brained integration, helping them to align physical sensations with emotional insights.

Outcomes:

Over the course of treatment, the teen who had spiraled into substance abuse experienced a significant reduction in reactive behaviors. As his internal critic and bully lenses softened, he began to access the wisdom of his heart, leading to improved emotional regulation and a reduction in self-destructive impulses. Meanwhile, the teen who was oriented toward academic recovery deepened his inner alignment and expanded his capacity for long-term planning. Both teens reported feeling more whole and connected, with the adaptive teen successfully transitioning to a vocational path and the other gradually reengaging with educational opportunities. This case demonstrates how GCT's integrated approach can transform similar physical traumas into divergent outcomes based on internal alignment and the re-centering of the heart's guidance. *GCT reveals something that is rarely touched on when treating PTSD. The success in treatment is largely contingent on premorbid adjustment—where someone is 'before' their trauma. Same age, same disability, but two distinctly different approaches to their recovery.*

## Clinical Application Points: Adolescent Amputation and Divergent Responses

### Key Assessment Insights:

- Pre-morbid adjustment profoundly influences trauma response trajectory
- Developmental stage (identity formation) shapes meaning-making after physical loss
- Assessment should identify both risk and protective factors for each teen

### Effective Interventions:

- **Comparative Process Analysis:** Use contrasting cases to identify specific resilience factors
- **Developmental Recalibration Protocol:** Adjust expectations and goals to account for interrupted development

- **Peer Integration Process:** Carefully structured peer support to normalize adaptation without reinforcing maladaptive coping

**Adaptations for Adolescents:**

- Modified language that respects adolescent developmental needs while promoting maturity
- Balance autonomy and appropriate dependence during physical recovery
- Concrete, practical tools with specific application to school and social contexts

**Family System Approach:**

- Assess and address family patterns that may reinforce or undermine recovery
- Provide psychoeducation about adolescent responses to trauma and loss
- Create structured family involvement that supports healthy development

## Case #8: Low-Functioning Sexual Abuse Teen Retrieving Her Meaning and Purpose

### Presenting Problem and Diagnostic Context

Case #8 a fourteen-year-old girl, with cognitive impairments reflected by an IQ in the low seventies, presented for mandated therapy after years of sustained sexual abuse by a family member. Deeply affected by the abuse, she exhibited profound self-blame—repeatedly verbalizing "Why me?" and "It's my fault!"—and engaged in self-harming behaviors and substance use as ways to displace her emotional pain. GCT assessments revealed that her internal landscape was dominated by rigid critic and mediator lenses, which reinforced feelings of worthlessness and isolation. Her low premorbid self-esteem and lack of adaptive self-care had left her vulnerable to external validation and chronic disconnection.

Treatment Process:

Establishing Rapport and Observer Activation:

Given her guarded and defiant behavior, the therapist's initial focus was on building trust through consistent, empathetic engagement. Mindfulness practices were introduced slowly to help her activate her internal Observer—learning to notice her thoughts and feelings without immediately engaging with them.

Creative Externalization of Self-Critical Narratives:

A pivotal intervention was the use of creative tools to externalize her internal self-criticism. Drawing on Gestalt Therapy techniques the therapist modified a pair of glasses, displaying her self-deprecating phrases onto cardboard lenses. Inserting them into the glasses frame, this method became a tangible exercise that enabled the client to see her words "Why me?" and "It's my fault!" as externalized narratives (blocking her vision) rather than intrinsic truths. Repeated exercises with these glasses helped her to gradually see the truth of her experience and eventually 'let go' of blinding negative messages.

Integrating CBT and DBT Techniques:

CBT was employed to help her identify and dispute distorted thoughts. At the same time, DBT mindfulness and distress tolerance skills provided her with strategies to manage overwhelming emotions. This dual approach enabled her to gradually dismantle the rigid internal narratives imposed by her critic lens.

Somatic and Expressive Modalities:

Given her cognitive challenges, the therapist integrated expressive art therapy and gentle somatic practices. Through drawing, guided imagery, and body-focused exercises, she was encouraged to express feelings that she could not articulate verbally. This process promoted a gradual reconnection with her body and emotions, fostering a more nuanced internal dialogue.

Outcomes:

After sustained intervention, the teen began to demonstrate noticeable shifts in her internal dialogue. The externalization exercises reduced the immediacy of her self-blame, allowing space for self-compassion to emerge. As her Observer became more active, she started to see the self-critical messages as distortions rather than immutable truths. Over time, she reported a decrease in self-harming behaviors and a reduced reliance on substances for coping. Although progress was gradual, she began to engage more openly in therapy, setting small goals for academic and social activities. Ultimately, the integration of creative reframing, mindfulness, and expressive modalities fostered a transformation from a state of deep vulnerability to one of emerging resilience and self-compassion

**Clinical Application Points: Cognitive Impairment and Sexual Trauma**

**Key Assessment Insights:**

- Cognitive limitations require modified assessment approaches that don't rely heavily on verbal processing

- Self-blame patterns may be more concrete and less amenable to cognitive interventions
- Assessment should identify strengths and capabilities, not just limitations

**Effective Interventions:**

- **Concrete Externalization Technique:** Use physical objects (like the modified glasses) to represent internal states
- **Simplified Observer Activation:** Use clear, concrete language to help client notice internal experiences
- **Repetition-Based Integration:** Create consistent, repeated practices that build procedural rather than declarative learning

**Adaptations for Cognitive Limitations:**

- Break concepts into smaller, concrete steps with immediate application
- Use visual aids, physical metaphors, and role-play instead of abstract discussion
- Extend the timeline for integration, allowing for more repetition and practice

**Trauma-Specific Considerations:**

- Address concrete safety concerns and boundary recognition
- Distinguish between developmental and trauma-related behaviors

- Create simple but effective self-regulation tools that don't require complex cognitive processing

**Case #9: Suicidal Interruption and the Gesture of Hope**

**Presenting Problem and Diagnostic Context**

Case #9 a 34-year-old man, struggling with clinical depression and substance dependence, had planned a suicide attempt. He drove to a secluded cabin with a fifth of Jack Daniels and his 45-caliber pistol in hand, prepared to end his life. He's unsure why he didn't follow-through or stopped?

Assessment and Internal Mapping:

Comprehensive GCT intake revealed his inner landscape was dominated by harsh egoic critic and bully lenses that fueled relentless self-blame and despair. In addition, psychodynamic assessments uncovered deep-seated attachment wounds and unresolved feelings of abandonment. His emotional thermometer indicated high reactivity and hyperarousal, while his capacity for inner resilience and an innate Observer was still latent but overshadowed by overwhelming distress.

Treatment Process:

Establishing Safety & Observer Activation:

Therapy began by creating a secure and nonjudgmental space. Mindfulness and grounding exercises were used to help him activate his internal Observer—allowing him to notice his thoughts and sensations without immediate identification with them.

Heart-Centered Narrative Reframing:

The therapist guided him to articulate and reframe his traumatic narrative. Creative imagery was employed to help him envision his heart as a compassionate, steady beacon—a guiding light that could illuminate hope even in the absence of physical sight.

Gestalt Methods:

Using Gestalt techniques, the therapist invited him to focus on the "here-and-now" of his bodily sensations. In one key session, he was asked to describe any physical movements he noticed, which led to the observation of him rubbing his four fingers and thumb together—a spontaneous gesture that indicated internal stirring. When his suicidal thoughts were interrupted by a phone call from his daughter he rubbed his fingers as stated: "I don't know. I stopped because something inside of me said that tomorrow might be just a little bit better." **This becomes a real-life example of the 'invisible something else' or 'matter of the heart' that emerges as a lubricant made by the clients blood, sweat, and tears. A sacred knowing that comes to the surface (with everyone) that softens the friction between one's ego and heart.*

Transpersonal Methods:

Guided meditations and reflective visualizations were introduced to help him access a sense of deeper, transcendent self. These practices encouraged him to connect with his inner "observer" that had been present since birth, suggesting that his pain might be part of a larger journey toward spiritual awakening and personal transformation.

Psychodynamic Exploration:

In parallel, psychodynamic techniques were employed to explore unconscious relational patterns and early attachment wounds. The therapist gently examined transference dynamics, helping him see how past experiences of abandonment and rejection contributed to his current state of despair. This insight allowed him to begin differentiating between reactive ego defenses and his authentic inner self.

Integration and Empowerment:

Over the course of treatment, these modalities were woven together. The external interruption—his daughter's phone call—had already served as a critical catalyst by momentarily halting his lethal plan. Building on that, the therapist helped him interpret his spontaneous gesture of rubbing his fingers as a symbolic expression of emerging hope and the "lubricant of compassion." As his Observer became more active and his heart's guidance emerged, he gradually integrated these insights into his self-concept, feeling empowered to envision a future beyond despair.

Outcomes:

By the end of the treatment course, the patient experienced a significant reduction in his symptoms and suicidal ideation. His thoughts quieted and decreased, and he reported feeling a renewed sense of self-worth and internal connection. The integration of mindfulness, Gestalt, transpersonal, and psychodynamic methods facilitated a profound shift—from overwhelming self-blame and isolation to a state where his internal Observer and heart-led wisdom began to guide him. Ultimately, he moved from a state of near-suicidal despair to one of emerging hope and empowerment, demonstrating the transformative potential of Gifted Compassionate Therapy.

## Clinical Application Points: Acute Suicidality and Existential Crisis

### Key Assessment Insights:

- Interrupted suicide attempt provides critical information about protective factors
- Physical gestures (finger rubbing) offer somatic access points for intervention
- Assessment should identify specific existential questions that preceded suicidal ideation

### Effective Interventions:

- **Crisis Stabilization Protocol:** Immediate safety planning with concrete steps and resources
- **Somatic Anchor Technique:** Use the spontaneous gesture (finger rubbing) as access point to hope
- **Existential Meaning Bridge:** Connect interrupted attempt to larger questions of purpose and meaning

### Risk Management Considerations:

- Develop comprehensive safety plan with multiple layers of support
- Identify and strengthen protective factors (daughter's connection)
- Create concrete structure for overwhelming emotional states

### Documentation Requirements:

- Thorough risk assessment documentation at each session

- Clear decision-making process for level-of-care determinations
- Specific plans for managing increased risk if it recurs

**Recovery Markers:**

- Transition from passive to active hope indicators
- Development of future-oriented perspective beyond immediate crisis
- Integration of suicidal impulse into meaningful narrative of transformation

## Reflections on GCT's Role in Action

GCT's holistic framework served as the unifying model throughout these diverse cases. In each instance, traditional modalities—CBT, DBT, IFS, somatic therapy, psychodynamic exploration, humanistic and existential approaches, and transpersonal practices—were integrated into a cohesive approach centered on the observer, heart, ego, and spirit. By addressing misalignment on every level, GCT transformed therapy from simple symptom management to a journey of intentional evolution, where each client learned to reconnect with their innate capacity for growth, self-compassion, and authentic connection.

*Reflective Prompt:*
In what ways does integrating multiple therapeutic modalities enhance the effectiveness of your work? How might you share the success stories of these cases with colleagues or clients to illustrate the transformative potential of GCT?

**Conclusion**

This chapter has bridged the theoretical underpinnings of Gifted Compassionate Therapy with its practical application through real-life cases. By demonstrating how GCT's comprehensive intake assessment, targeted interventions, and integrated therapeutic approaches can transform lives, we have shown that alignment is not a distant ideal but an attainable state that reduces suffering and fosters intentional evolution.

Key takeaways include:

- The importance of a holistic intake that maps the client's internal landscape.
- How core misalignments—such as dominant egoic lenses—can be identified and reframed through a combination of established and innovative therapeutic tools.
- The transformative impact of integrating modalities (CBT, DBT, IFS, somatic, psychodynamic, humanistic, existential, and transpersonal approaches) with GCT's framework.
- The ripple effects of personal transformation on relationships, community engagement, and systemic change.

As you move forward, consider how the insights from these cases might inform you of your own practice. The real-life applications presented here are intended not only to illustrate therapeutic techniques but also to inspire you to envision a world where intentional evolution and heart-centered living become the norm.

# Chapter Nine
# Societal Implications of GCT

**Introduction**

Gifted Compassionate Therapy (GCT) is not merely a framework for personal healing—it is a call to action for cultural and societal transformation. In a world increasingly dominated by egoic systems and fear-based structures, GCT offers an alternative path: a shift toward compassion, alignment, and reciprocity. This chapter explores how GCT's principles extend beyond the therapy room to reimagine societal norms, challenge the limitations of diagnosis-heavy approaches, and foster a culture where individuals are truly seen, valued, and empowered to grow.

At its core, GCT challenges conventional mental health care. Whereas diagnostic labels often reduce individuals to their symptoms, GCT reframes these labels as signposts on a broader journey of intentional evolution. This chapter examines how rethinking diagnostic labels and egoic systems can lead to a more humane society—one where personal transformation has ripple effects in education, healthcare, workplace cultures, and governance.

*Transitional Note:*
As you complete this book, consider not only how GCT transforms individual lives but also how these changes can inspire systemic transformation. Each section builds toward a

comprehensive vision for cultural change that is rooted in heart-centered alignment.

## 8.1 From Egoic to Humane Systems

### Reframing Diagnostic Labels and the Mental Health Paradigm

For decades, mental health care has been shaped by the DSM diagnostic system, a framework that categorizes human experiences into specific disorders. Although these labels serve critical clinical and research functions, they often activate stigma and limit self-perception. Research shows that diagnostic labels frequently trigger stereotypes and negative self-assessments, which may lead to isolation and a diminished sense of worth (Hinshaw & Stier, 2008; Schulze, 2007).

GCT challenges this reductionist view by recognizing that while diagnoses are useful tools, they are not the whole story. Clients are more than the sum of their symptoms. By moving beyond the limitations of a label-driven model, GCT invites individuals to reconnect with their inherent humanity. In doing so, it paves the way for a narrative of growth, intentional evolution, and genuine self-compassion.

### The Cost of Egoic Systems

The influence of egoic systems extends beyond individual clinical settings. Cultural structures—shaped by consumerism, competition, and the need for control—mirror the DSM's reductionist approach. These systems often value external metrics such as wealth and productivity over authentic human connection and well-being (Pescosolido et al., 2010). Just as clients feel fragmented when reduced to a diagnosis, society suffers from disconnection and dehumanization. You know now that this is an Egosolarism problem

GCT challenges these prevailing structures by urging us to reframe success, identity, and worth. Rather than measuring value solely by external achievements, GCT emphasizes alignment with the heart. When the heart guides, values such as compassion, connection, and mutual respect become the true markers of success.

*Reflective Prompt:*
Consider how diagnostic labels have affected your own self-perception or that of your clients. In what ways could reframing these labels as tools for growth lead to a more humane approach in your practice?

## 8.2 Cultural Transformation

### Shifting from Fear-Based to Compassion-Driven Frameworks

In our current fear-based culture, individuals are conditioned to protect themselves through judgment, control, and avoidance. These defensive patterns, deeply rooted in ego dysfunction, are evident at all levels—from personal relationships to global institutions. Fear, rather than fostering collaboration, breeds competition and hierarchy (Corrigan et al., 2012).

GCT envisions a paradigm shift: a society built on reciprocity, compassion, and intentional evolution. Just as GCT helps clients align their observer, ego, spirit, and heart, it offers a model for transforming cultural systems. Consider the following applications:

- **Education:**
  Rather than categorizing students as "gifted," "learning disabled," or "at risk," a GCT-informed education system

would focus on nurturing each student's unique strengths and fostering self-compassion and intrinsic motivation.

- **Healthcare:**
  The biomedical model, with its focus on symptom management, could be enriched by GCT's integrative approach that treats patients as whole people—honoring mind, body, and spirit.
- **Workplace Cultures:**
  Instead of prioritizing productivity and conformity, organizations could adopt GCT's principles to foster environments that support individual growth, collaboration, and sustainable well-being.
- **Community and Governance:**
  Fear-based policies breed division. In contrast, compassionate and reciprocal frameworks can help communities build networks of trust and shared responsibility.

### Addressing the Stigma of Diagnostic Labels

Stigma is one of the most insidious effects of traditional diagnostic practices. Labels can lead to negative self-perceptions and reduced expectations for recovery (Hinshaw & Stier, 2008; Schulze, 2007). GCT directly confronts this challenge by reframing diagnoses as useful signposts on the journey toward alignment rather than as definitive labels.

- **Reframing Diagnoses as Tools:**
  GCT encourages clients to see diagnoses as one aspect of their story, not as a fixed identity.

- **Emphasizing the Whole Person:**
  Rather than reducing individuals to symptoms, GCT focuses on the person's essence, potential, and capacity for growth.
- **Collaborative Healing:**
  By involving clients in the diagnostic process, GCT fosters a shared language of healing and empowers individuals to reclaim their narrative.

*Reflective Prompt:*
How might the removal of stigma around diagnostic labels transform the therapeutic experience for your clients? What language can you use to help clients see their diagnoses as opportunities for growth?

## 8.3 The Promise and Challenges of Holistic Mental Health Care

### A New Paradigm for Healing and Growth

The demand for holistic mental health care reflects a growing recognition that healing must address the whole person—mind, body, and spirit. While holistic approaches promise a more integrated form of care, their implementation often falls short. Research indicates that, despite positive rhetoric, many holistic methods are applied superficially, leaving clients disappointed (Gaudiano et al., 2021).

GCT bridges this gap by providing a structured, integrative framework that unites diverse modalities into a cohesive whole. By aligning the observer, heart, ego, and spirit, GCT not only reduces suffering but also empowers clients to live more authentically and compassionately (Vecchio, 2025).A perspective that accepts the ego was never meant to be the center of the human condition.

## The Benefits of Holistic Approaches

When implemented effectively, holistic care can:

- Improve overall mental well-being and reduce symptoms of depression, anxiety, and stress (Sarris et al., 2019).
- Enhance interpersonal communication and family dynamics.
- Support recovery from addiction and manage chronic pain and trauma (Lake & Turner, 2017).

GCT's strength lies in its ability to integrate these benefits into a model that treats clients as whole, evolving beings rather than as collections of symptoms. In the end, this evolves consciousness.

## Barriers to Holistic Implementation

Despite its promise, holistic care faces significant obstacles:

- **Lack of Integration:**
  Health services often operate in silos, separating mental from physical care.
- **Time Constraints:**
  The need for rapid results can conflict with the slow, reflective process required for holistic healing.
- **Insufficient Training:**
  Many practitioners are not adequately trained in integrative approaches, hindering effective implementation.

GCT addresses these barriers by:

1. **Mind-Body-Spirit Integration:**
   Embedding integrative practices into treatment plans for a more complete picture of well-being (Lake et al., 2021).
2. **Comprehensive Training:**
   Advocating for practitioner education in holistic and psychospiritual approaches (Rosenbaum et al., 2020).
3. **Interdisciplinary Collaboration:**
   Promoting teams that include mental health, physical health, and spiritual care professionals.
4. **Policy Support:**
   Suggesting changes to incentivize holistic care practices on a systemic level.

*Reflective Prompt:*
What practical strategies have you seen that bridge the gap between holistic theory and practice? How might interdisciplinary collaboration enhance your approach?

### The Misuse of "Holistic" as a Buzzword

Too often, "holistic" is used as a buzzword without genuine integration. Clients may become skeptical when superficial approaches fail to deliver real change. GCT distinguishes itself by providing a detailed, authentic model that fully incorporates mind, body, and spirit into every intervention (Vecchio, 2025).

*Reflective Prompt:*
How can you ensure that holistic practices in your work are meaningful rather than merely buzzwords? What measures would you use to evaluate the depth of integration in your interventions?

## 8.4 Bridging the Gap: Toward True Holistic Care

### Toward a Unified Model

To close the gap between the promise of holistic care and its current fragmented practice, several strategies can be employed:

1. **Mind-Body-Spirit Integration:**
   Embed integrative practices into every aspect of care, ensuring that interventions address all dimensions of the human experience.
2. **Comprehensive Training:**
   Equip practitioners with the skills and knowledge needed to implement true holistic care.
3. **Interdisciplinary Teams:**
   Develop collaborative teams that work together seamlessly to provide comprehensive care.
4. **Policy Support:**
   Advocate for systemic changes that incentivize and support holistic approaches.

GCT exemplifies these strategies by offering a structured model that emphasizes collaboration, self-awareness, and intentional evolution. Its humane spectrum framework, combined with tools like the observer and heart lens, ensures that every client is seen as a whole person, capable of growth beyond their symptoms (Vecchio, 2025).

*Visual Aid Suggestion:*
Consider a flowchart or table that summarizes these strategies alongside real-life examples from practice, highlighting the transition from fragmented to integrated care.

*Reflective Prompt:*
How might you adapt your current practice to foster a more holistic approach? What changes in policy or team structure could further support this shift?

**Conclusion: GCT as the Future of Holistic Care**

In a world where mental health care is often dominated by symptom-focused, reductionist models, Gifted Compassionate Therapy offers a transformative alternative. GCT's approach not only addresses individual suffering through a comprehensive, heart-centered framework but also holds the promise of reshaping cultural and societal norms. We have yet to make the existential shift that is now Galileo's unfinished lesson.

By reframing diagnostic labels, emphasizing the whole person, and advocating for collaborative, integrative care, GCT provides a blueprint for a more humane and connected society. Its principles encourage a shift from fear-based to compassion-driven systems, where the true worth of an individual is measured by alignment, authenticity, and reciprocal connection.

**Key Takeaways:**

- **Reframing Labels:**
  Moving beyond DSM categories to recognize diagnoses as tools for growth rather than definitive identities.
- **Cultural Transformation:**
  Embracing a holistic approach in education, healthcare, workplaces, and governance to promote connection and well-being.
- **Systemic Impact:**
  The ripple effects of individual alignment can transform

communities and organizations, fostering a more humane society.

- **Collaboration and Integration:**
  The future of mental health care lies in integrated, interdisciplinary approaches that honor the full spectrum of human experience.

**Reflective Prompt:**
Reflect on your own practice or community. What small change could you initiate that would begin to shift a fear-based system toward one of compassionate, holistic care?

**Future Directions and Research Implications:** Emerging research in neuroplasticity, heart coherence, and trauma-informed care will continue to inform and refine integrative approaches like GCT. As these fields evolve, so too will the practical applications of GCT, paving the way for innovative interventions and broader systemic change.

**Final Transitional Note:**
As you move forward, let the insights from this chapter inspire you to envision and contribute to a future in which mental health care is as holistic and integrated as the human beings it serves. GCT is not just a model for personal healing—it is a call to create a more compassionate, connected world. Life in a humane universe is a choice!

## 8.5 Practical Recommendations for Implementing GCT at the Systemic Level

### 1. Introducing GCT Principles in Staff Meetings and Training Sessions

**Structured Mini-Workshops:**

- Develop 15-20 minute modules on core GCT concepts like "The Observer" or "Heart-Centered Alignment" that can be integrated into existing staff meetings
- Begin with experiential exercises (e.g., a brief mindfulness practice to activate the observer) before introducing theoretical concepts
- Create accessible handouts with visual representations of key GCT frameworks, like the alignment equation ($E + Hc = \downarrow S$)

**Peer Consultation Format:**

- Establish a monthly case consultation group where clinicians can discuss challenging cases through the GCT lens
- Use a structured format: 10 minutes for case presentation, 10 minutes for identifying egoic patterns and heart disconnection, 10 minutes for intervention planning
- Rotate leadership roles to build institutional capacity and shared ownership of the approach

**Integration with Existing Frameworks:**

- Map connections between GCT and already-accepted approaches (e.g., trauma-informed care, mindfulness-based interventions)
- Highlight complementary aspects rather than positioning GCT as replacing current practices

- Demonstrate how GCT enhances rather than competes with evidence-based practices

**2. Effective Language and Approaches for Administrators and Policy Makers**

**Translating Terminology:**

- Reframe GCT concepts using language familiar to administrators (e.g., "holistic assessment" instead of "observer activation")
- Connect GCT outcomes to metrics administrators already value, such as reduced readmission rates, improved client satisfaction, or decreased staff burnout
- Develop one-page executive summaries highlighting key benefits and implementation costs

**Data-Driven Advocacy:**

- Collect preliminary outcome data from your practice showing improvements in client wellbeing using GCT approaches
- Present cost-effectiveness arguments (e.g., holistic intake assessments may take longer initially but result in more targeted interventions and fewer sessions overall)
- Highlight research on the financial impact of employee wellbeing programs based on similar principles

**Collaborative Approach:**

- Invite administrators to experience rather than just hear about GCT through brief experiential exercises

- Propose pilot projects with clear evaluation metrics rather than system-wide overhauls
- Form alliances with other departments (e.g., employee wellness, quality improvement) to strengthen proposals

**3. Small-Scale Initiatives to Model GCT Principles**

**Redesign Physical Spaces:**

- Create a "heart-centered" consultation room where clinicians can practice GCT techniques
- Add visual reminders (e.g., posters showing the observer-spirit-ego-heart framework) in staff areas
- Designate quiet spaces for mindfulness practices that support observer activation

**Documentation Reforms:**

- Develop intake assessment templates that incorporate GCT's holistic components
- Create progress note formats that track alignment and heart-centered shifts alongside symptomatic changes
- Introduce "alignment language" in treatment plans that emphasizes the client's whole-person journey

**Community Building:**

- Establish a "Compassion Circle" where staff can practice heart-centered communication
- Implement brief "alignment check-ins" at the beginning of team meetings

- Create opportunities for staff to share personal experiences with GCT principles

### 4. Examples of Successful Advocacy Efforts and Case Studies

**Healthcare Organization Case Study:** "Memorial Wellness Center implemented GCT principles by first establishing a pilot program in their outpatient mental health department. They began by training ten clinicians in the GCT approach, particularly focusing on holistic assessment and heart-centered interventions. After six months, they documented a 23% reduction in client cancellations, a 17% decrease in medication adjustments, and significantly improved staff satisfaction scores. These results provided the leverage needed to expand the program throughout their behavioral health services."

**Educational Setting Example:** "Riverview High School incorporated elements of GCT into their student support services through a 'Whole-Student' initiative. School counselors adopted the observer-heart framework when working with struggling students, helping them recognize egoic patterns of self-criticism and perfectionism. After one academic year, disciplinary referrals decreased by 31%, and student self-reported wellbeing scores improved significantly. The program has since expanded to include teacher training on heart-centered classroom management."

**Workplace Wellness Success:** "Tech-Forward, a mid-sized software company, addressed rising employee burnout by implementing GCT-based wellness practices. They created daily 'observer moments'—brief mindfulness periods—and redesigned performance reviews to incorporate heart-centered feedback alongside traditional metrics. After nine months, they reported a

26% reduction in sick days, improved retention rates, and measurable increases in team cohesion scores."

**5. Tools for Measuring and Documenting GCT Impact**

**Assessment Instruments:**

- Develop a "Humane Spectrum Scale" to measure shifts in alignment before and after implementing GCT approaches
- Create an "Organizational Alignment Index" to assess institutional environments
- Adapt existing wellbeing measures to incorporate GCT components

**Implementation Tracking:**

- Design a phased implementation checklist for organizations adopting GCT principles
- Create process evaluation tools to monitor fidelity to GCT approaches during the transition
- Develop observation protocols for supervisors to provide feedback on clinicians' use of GCT techniques

**Impact Documentation:**

- Establish a multi-dimensional outcome framework that tracks:
    - Client symptom reduction
    - Client-reported alignment and heart connection
    - Staff engagement and reduced burnout

  - System-level metrics (e.g., reduced crisis interventions, shorter treatment duration)

- Create case study templates that capture qualitative shifts in organizational culture
- Implement periodic "alignment audits" to identify areas where ego-centered practices persist

**Practical Measurement Protocol:**

1. Baseline assessment of current organizational practices
2. Implementation of targeted GCT interventions
3. 3-month, 6-month, and 12-month reassessment
4. Comparison with similar departments or organizations not using GCT approaches
5. Documentation of both quantitative and qualitative outcomes

By implementing these practical recommendations, therapists and organizations can move beyond individual application of GCT to create systemic change that fosters heart-centered alignment throughout their communities and institutions.

# Epilogue
# A Measurable, Evidence-Based Path to Intentional Evolution

In my years of clinical practice and research, I have come to see that the principles behind Gifted Compassionate Therapy (GCT) are not merely abstract metaphors—they are grounded in measurable, observable realities. I have gathered empirical evidence from thousands of trauma patients, and through rigorous assessment, I have seen how the interplay between the ego and the heart can be quantified, monitored, and ultimately transformed. This model, which I call Intentional Evolution, and its resulting liberation Gifted Compassionate Therapy, represents a new and evidence-based pathway to healing that transcends traditional, ego-centric approaches.

**1. Not Just Metaphors—Observable Realities**

I have discovered that the formulas I propose—$E^2 - Hc = \uparrow S$ (where an exaggerated ego minus the heart as compass results in increased suffering) and $E + Hc = \downarrow S$ (where a balanced ego combined with the heart's guidance leads to decreased suffering)—are not abstract ideas. They are evidence that consciousness can, in fact, evolve. They are rooted in data derived from clinical assessments, including head–heart–gut evaluations, developmental life stage measurements, analyses of self-care methods, and affective pairing assessments. In my work, these measures are not just symbolic; they represent real, quantifiable dynamics of the human psyche. **Where the stagnation of an evolving consciousness is the result of a failed existential shift – Egosolarism.**

### 2. Quantifiable Interplay of Ego and Heart

Through standardized tests and projective assessments, I have been able to measure the dynamic relationship between the ego and the heart. This model provides a foundational framework—or a "skeleton," if you will—that gains depth through individual data. Just as medical professionals rely on diagnostic imaging to reveal the truth beneath the surface, my approach uses quantifiable metrics to show how the ego's distortions and the heart's clarity interact. The consistency of this data across diverse trauma survivors convinces me that these formulas are applicable across different cultural, gender, and racial contexts.

### 3. Standardized Interpretation of Inter-Subjective Experiences

Although the realm of inter-subjective experience can seem inherently variable, I have found that the methods I use for measurement are remarkably standardized. Much like an X-ray that reliably identifies a tumor regardless of individual differences, my model offers **a universal lens to understand the division within the ego and its profound impact on human suffering**. This standardization ensures that my approach is scientifically reliable and practically applicable.

### 4. Spiritual Gravity as an Observable Phenomenon

One of the most compelling insights I've encountered is that what I call "spiritual gravity" is not merely an analogy—it is an observable, measurable phenomenon. I have seen that individuals are born unified and emotionally whole; yet, through experiences of guilt, shame, and trauma, the ego gradually creates a divide. This division produces a kind of gravitational pull that warps the psyche and leads to suffering. By measuring these shifts, I can demonstrate that **the concept of spiritual gravity is both empirically grounded and therapeutically relevant. Galileo would say, "We need only to look up, then look in."**

### 5. A Restored Bridge to Deeper Psychological Truths

Ultimately, my work with GCT is built on the timeless truth that "what you believe, you become." Unlike approaches that focus solely on cognitive restructuring, my model emphasizes the psyche's inherent self-correcting capacity. By restoring the heart as the central compass and addressing the core imbalance caused by ego solarism, I've helped severe trauma patients move beyond merely managing symptoms. They numbered into the thousands, where each embarked on a transformative journey toward authentic healing and personal evolution.

### Conclusion

In reflecting on my journey and the evidence I have gathered, I am convinced that Intentional Evolution and Gifted Compassionate Therapy offers a measurable, evidence-based path to healing. By re-centering the heart and aligning the observer, spirit, and ego, this model not only reduces suffering but also facilitates genuine psychological growth. It transcends 'life as it is' and firmly places us on a path of 'life as intended. It provides answers to the existential "what" and "why" we are, something that has long been neglected by traditional therapeutic models.. We no longer have to imagine a mental health world that is universal and free of stigma.

In this context, I have learned that living in a humane universe is a conscious choice—one that rejects reductionist, ego-driven systems in favor of a more compassionate, integrative approaches. My hope is that this philosophy and model will inspire clinicians and clients alike to embrace intentional evolution as a transformative pathway toward lasting, meaningful change. We no longer have to imagine an evolving consciousness; we need only shift our perspective—and begin!

# References

Adler, A. (1956). *The individual psychology of Alfred Adler.* Basic Books.

American Psychiatric Association. (2013). *Diagnostic and statistical manual of mental disorders* (5th ed.). American Psychiatric Publishing.

Beck, A. T. (1976). *Cognitive therapy and the emotional disorders.* International Universities Press.

Berne, E. (1964). *Games people play: The basic handbook of transactional analysis.* Grove Press.

Bowlby, J. (1988). *A secure base: Parent-child attachment and healthy human development.* Basic Books.

Boyatzis, R. E., Smith, M. L., & Blaize, N. (2002). Developing sustainable leaders through coaching and compassion. *Academy of Management Executive, 16*(1), 143–156.

Chaplin, T. M. (2015). Emotion expression in children: A review. *Developmental Review, 36*, 1–33.

Christakis, N. A., & Fowler, J. H. (2013). *Social network effects on health: New perspectives and evidence.* Oxford University Press.

Clark, D. A., & Beck, A. T. (2010). *Cognitive therapy of anxiety disorders: Science and practice.* Guilford Press.

Corrigan, P. W., Druss, B. G., & Perlick, D. A. (2012). The impact of mental illness stigma on seeking and participating in mental health care. *Psychological Science in the Public Interest, 15*(2), 37–70.

Damasio, A. (2021). *Feeling & knowing: Making minds conscious.* Pantheon Books.

Dana, D. (2018). *The polyvagal theory in therapy: Engaging the rhythm of regulation.* W.W. Norton & Company.

Ekman, P. (2007). *Emotions revealed: Recognizing faces and feelings to improve communication and emotional life* (2nd ed.). Holt Paperbacks.

Freud, S. (1917/1957). *Introductory lectures on psychoanalysis.* Norton.

Gaudiano, B. A., et al. (2021). Implementing holistic approaches in mental health: A review of challenges and best practices. *Journal of Holistic Psychology, 18*(3), 215–230.

Geller, S. M., & Greenberg, L. S. (2012). *Therapeutic presence: A mindful approach to effective therapy.* American Psychological Association.

Goleman, D. (1998). *Working with emotional intelligence.* Bantam Books.

Grant, B. F., et al. (2008). Prevalence, correlates, and comorbidity of DSM-IV personality disorders: Results from the Wave 2 National Epidemiologic Survey on Alcohol and Related Conditions. *Journal of Clinical Psychiatry, 69*(7), 1033–1045.

Hanson, R., & Mendius, R. (2018). *Buddha's brain: The practical neuroscience of happiness, love, and wisdom.* New Harbinger Publications.

Heller, L., & LaPierre, A. (2012). *Healing developmental trauma: How early trauma affects self-regulation, self-image, and the capacity for relationship.* North Atlantic Books.

Jacobson, N. S., et al. (2001). Behavioral activation treatment for depression: Returning to contextual roots. *Clinical Psychology: Science and Practice.*

Jung, C. G. (1968). *The archetypes and the collective unconscious* (R. F. C. Hull, Trans.). Princeton University Press.

Kinderman, P., et al. (2013). The challenges of integrating holistic and biomedical models in healthcare. *Psychiatric Bulletin, 37*(6), 280–284.

Kobylińska, D., & Kusev, P. (2019). Emotional experience across cultures. *Journal of Cross-Cultural Psychology, 50*(3), 419–432.

Lausen, C., & Schacht, A. (2018). Gender differences in emotional recognition. *Journal of Social Psychology, 158*(4), 489–503.

Lake, F., & Turner, A. (2017). Bridging mental and physical health: The role of integrative approaches. *International Journal of Integrated Care, 17*(4), 1–10.

Levine, P. A. (2010). *In an unspoken voice: How the body releases trauma and restores goodness.* North Atlantic Books.

Linehan, M. M. (1993). *Cognitive-behavioral treatment of borderline personality disorder.* Guilford Press.

McCraty, R., & Zayas, M. A. (2014). Cardiac coherence, self-regulation, autonomic stability, and psychosocial well-being. *Frontiers in Psychology, 5*, 1090. https://doi.org/10.3389/fpsyg.2014.01090

McCraty, R., Atkinson, M., & Tomasino, D. (2015). *Science of the heart: Exploring the role of the heart in human performance.* Institute of HeartMath Research.

McGilchrist, I. (2019). *The master and his emissary: The divided brain and the making of the western world.* Yale University Press.

Mayer, E. A. (2016). *The mind-gut connection: How the hidden conversation within our bodies impacts our mood, our choices, and our overall health*. Harper Wave.

Neff, K. D. (2003). Self-compassion: An alternative conceptualization of a healthy attitude toward oneself. *Self and Identity, 2*(2), 85–101.

Ogden, P., Minton, K., & Pain, C. (2006). *Trauma and the body: A sensorimotor approach to psychotherapy*. W. W. Norton.

Perls, F., Hefferline, R., & Goodman, P. (1951). *Gestalt therapy: Excitement and growth in the human personality*. Julian Press.

Pescosolido, B. A., et al. (2010). A network analysis of mental health stigma and public attitudes. *American Journal of Public Health, 100*(12), 2342–2348.

Porges, S. W. (2017). *The pocket guide to the polyvagal theory: The transformative power of feeling safe*. W.W. Norton & Company.

Rogers, C. R. (1961). *On becoming a person: A therapist's view of psychotherapy*. Houghton Mifflin.

Schwartz, R. (1995). *Internal family systems therapy*. Guilford Press.

Shedler, J. (2010). The efficacy of psychodynamic psychotherapy. *American Psychologist, 65*(2), 98–109.

Siegel, D. J. (2019). *Aware: The science and practice of presence*. Tarcher Perigee.

Siegel, D. J. (2020). *The developing mind: How relationships and the brain interact to shape who we are* (3rd ed.). Guilford Press.

Simon, R. W., & Nath, L. E. (2004). Gender and emotion in the workplace: A multi-study analysis. *Journal of Management, 30*(2), 243–268.

Stinson, F. S., et al. (2008). Prevalence, correlates, disability, and comorbidity of DSM-IV narcissistic personality disorder. *Journal of Clinical Psychiatry, 69*(7), 1033–1045.

Tangney, J. P. (2000). Humility, shame, and guilt. In R. Baumeister (Ed.), *The guilty mind: The psychology of shame, morality, and social regulation* (pp. 95–117). Guilford Press.

Van der Kolk, B. (2014). *The body keeps the score: Brain, mind, and body in the healing of trauma*. Viking.

Vecchio, E. L. (2020). *Feelings and reason: Activating your heart as compass despite the ego's interference*. Best Publishing.

Vecchio, E. L. (2025). *The soul's wisdom: Five questions that shape our lives*. Life in a Humane Universe.

Vecchio, E. L. (2025). *Galileo's unfinished lesson: How ego distorted human evolution and how we fix it*. Life in a Humane Universe.

Walsh, R., & Vaughan, F. (1993). *Paths beyond ego: The transpersonal vision*. Tarcher.

Wachtel, P. L. (2011). *Therapeutic communication: Knowing what to say when* (2nd ed.). Guilford Press.

Made in the USA
Columbia, SC
17 March 2025

55185940R00133